RELEVANT DISCIPLESHIP™
RESOURCE MANUAL

...resources for practicing the disciplines of a disciple

Relevant Ministry, Inc.

Relevant Ministry Publishing

Gulfport, MS, United States

ISBN-13: 978-0692997987
ISBN-10: 0692997989

Relevant Ministry Publishing
Gulfport, MS
United States

www.relevantministry.org

Book layout, cover art and design by Kaila McBride.

contents

introduction

We want to thank those who have walked alongside us on this spiritual journey ... from the first fourteen men who experienced one-to-one discipleship with Nelson to the thirty women who helped Pam pilot a group model for churches; and the multitude of personal one-to-one discipleship and coach training connections Relevant Ministry has had with people around the world. The outcome has not only been spiritual development in all of our lives; but also, the development of Relevant Discipleship™.

Our goal in the beginning of this journey was to discover the answers to several questions; primarily, "How could discipleship be an intentional, ongoing, transformational process?" And, "How could a discipleship process truly multiply, where disciples make disciples who make disciples?"

We also discovered there were two significant barriers which needed to be overcome for most people to feel confident to begin their journey of discipleship ... "What do I do?" and "What do I say?" As a result, The Relevant Discipleship Pathway™ and Nehemiah Response Coaching Model™ were developed as discipleship tools; resulting in transformation in the lives of Christ followers who experienced Relevant Discipleship™.

We are still on the journey and we're glad you are a part of the journey of discipleship. We pray this resource manual will help you with your next step of being a disciple of Jesus Christ and then becoming a disciple maker for Christ!

Disciplee:

Since you are holding this resource manual in your hands, we know you are ready to embark on the most incredible journey ... the journey of discipleship. Relevant Discipleship™ is an intentional, ongoing, transformational process. This is not a program about discipleship, this is a personal experience of developing an intimate relationship with the living God. You will soon discover that Relevant Discipleship™ is more about "being" rather than "doing." Relevant Discipleship™ is genuinely a "way of life for the rest of your life."

Over the next six months, you will meet regularly with your disciple maker either every two or three weeks. Each discipleship session, you will have an opportunity to share how God showed up around one of the 7 disciplines you will be focusing on for that period of time. Remember, Relevant Discipleship™ is a process, not a program. You don't have boxes to check off ... this is about you and your relationship with God. Your only goal is to weave the discipline you are focusing on into every aspect of your life ... relationally, responsively, and how you reveal Christ to others. As you continue, make room for the Holy Spirit to work; and, you will experience transformation in your life.

Disciple maker:

Since you have experienced Relevant Discipleship™ as a disciple, now you have the privilege to walk alongside another Christ follower using the coaching approach to discipleship. God has entrusted you with this opportunity to disciple someone by being an authentic, prayerful, devoted follower of Christ. You will at times sense the responsibility of discipleship and you will also be able to share in the rewards of seeing transformation in the life of the disciple you are coming alongside.

Within the Relevant Discipleship™ Resource Manual, you will find a page of instructions dedicated to each of the three sections of resources ... **articles, coaching tools, and lessons.** You will also find an appendix containing an answer key to the lessons and helpful discipleship tools.

Suggested one-to-one discipleship session flow for the disciple maker:

- Several days before you meet, confirm your session date, time, and place.
- Use the Nehemiah Response Coaching Model™ to help guide your conversation. Begin by asking, "Where would you like to start today?"
- Engage and ask questions about his/her experience around the discipline he/she chose to focus on for the past two or three weeks. "How did you see God show up?"
- Ask, "What thoughts did the devotional articles or coaching tool stimulate around the discipline you have been focusing on?"

- Work through the suggested (∗) discipleship lesson, unless your disciplee is part of a group or class where the lessons are being taught.
- Ask, "What are your thoughts around the lesson and how might you apply this lesson to your life?"
- Pick the next discipline to focus on. Share that the other disciplines you have previously focused on will not be disregarded. The purpose behind the focus on one discipline is to learn and grow in that area during the two or three weeks. Ultimately, a growing disciple will experience a balance of all 7 disciplines at all times.
- Point out too, the disciplines are not a set of actions to check-off each day. Rather, practicing the disciplines are about making room to experience God.

Next steps: Following a Train the Discipler™ Workshop

- Meet one-to-one using the articles and coaching tool for the discipline you are currently focusing on.
- If one-to-one discipleship is part of your group or class, when you meet, you can use the 12 lessons to reinforce the one-to-one discipleship happening outside of the group or class.
- If you're not in a group or class, use the 7 suggested lessons (∗) out of the 12 lessons during your one-to-one discipleship sessions.

If you are starting the Relevant Discipleship™ process before holding a Train the Discipler™ Workshop, use the 'Before you begin' resource in the lesson section on pages 90 to 93 for an introductory session with your disciplee.

Training Videos:

Short training videos for disciple makers are available on the following webpage, www.relevantministry.org/relevantdiscipleship. There are footnotes with the web address at the bottom of the Introductory one-to-one session, all 7 coaching tools, and the 7 suggested lessons (∗) out of the 12 lessons.

articles

Instructions:

In this section of the resource manual, you will find articles by the Relevant Ministry team specifically written to enrich both personal and spiritual development by practicing the 7 disciplines. There are four articles for each of the 7 disciplines. Each article is two pages and can be read to stimulate thought and bring encouragement. The first article is about the discipline in general. Then, the following three articles connect the particular discipline to each of the 3Rs - Relational, Responsive and Reveals Christ.

Perhaps as you read the articles, the Holy Spirit will remind you about a comparable article, devotional or book you have read in the past. Use these nudges from the Holy Spirit throughout the time you are focusing on a particular discipline to be challenged in your spiritual walk. Purposefully, become more aware of how you might incorporate the discipline into your life as a habit.

Remember, practicing the 7 disciplines is not a mundane checklist where you check it off when you complete the task. Instead, Relevant Discipleship™ is an intentional process where you make room for God, allowing the work of the Holy Spirit to bring about transformation in your life.

Here's a brief description of each of the 7 disciplines including its relationship to scripture found in the early church of Acts and the seven churches of Revelation:

WORSHIP – experiencing God when gathered with other believers and through the week as a lifestyle

"praising God" Acts 2:47

Ephesus, *"forsaken their first love"* Revelation 2:4

PRAYER – communicating with God alone and with others

"They devoted themselves - to the breaking of bread and to prayer" Acts 2:42

Smyrna, *"don't be afraid - the devil will put some of you in prison to test you - be faithful"* Revelation 2:10

WORD – developing a deep relationship with God and having passion to know him more

"They devoted themselves to the apostles' teaching" Acts 2:42

Pergamos, *"compromised their faith and needed to repent"* Revelation 2:16

MINISTRY – discovering spiritual gifts and serving like Christ

"to give to anyone who had need" Acts 2:45

Thyatira, *"loved the world and concerned about self"* Revelation 2:20

DISCIPLESHIP – growing godly in character with a foundation of personal values and purpose

"They devoted themselves" Acts 2:42

Sardis, *"fallen asleep and just going through the motions"* Revelation 3:2

COMMUNITY – loving one another and sharing life

"They devoted themselves - to fellowship" Acts 2:42

Philadelphia, *"had an open door"* Revelation 3:8 (philea = brotherly love)

EVANGELISM – cultivating intentional friendships with not yet believers

The early church was *"enjoying the favor of all the people. And the
Lord added to their number daily those who were being saved"* Acts 2:47

The church at Laodecia was, *"lukewarm - self-sufficient and inward focused"* Revelation 3:16

What do I really love most?
by Jeff Hegstrom

In their book, *Worship: Rediscovering the Missing Jewel*, Allen and Borror describe worship as, "An active response to God in which we declare his worth!" (page 16)
How would you describe worship?

Most of us have preconceived ideas of what we think worship is. How many of you have thought about worship as: music, singing, emotions, feelings, an experience, or a Sunday morning church service? What other thoughts come to mind?

What does worship mean to you?	**What describes true worship in the life of a believer?**

If you're serious about wanting to draw closer to God, a committed life of worship is essential. A life without worship to God is not optional for a believer!

True worship is what God desires of his creation:

> Exodus 20:3-5, *"Do not worship any god except me. Do not make idols that look like anything in the sky or on earth or in the ocean under the earth. Don't bow down and worship idols. I am the Lord your God, and I demand all your love."*- CEV

> Matthew 22:37-38, *"Jesus replied, 'Love the Lord your God with all your heart, and with all your soul, and with your mind. This is the first and greatest commandment.'"* – NIV

We were created to worship and love God; but sometimes, we choose something or someone else to worship. It might be money, career, fame, material items, a significant other, ourselves ... and the list goes on. When we worship anything other than God, we are sinning by disobeying his first and greatest commandment - *"to love him."* Plus, we are failing to do the very thing he created us to do.

In order to truly understand what we are created for; we need to understand that worship is an active response to God.

> *"Authentic worship is a response to an authentic encounter with the living God. When we worship God, we declare his worth. But in order to declare the worth of God, we must first discover his worth."*
>
> (Buddy Owens, Editorial Director of Purpose Driven Ministries: Saddleback Church)

First, how would you describe God's worth?

And, what does it mean to you to declare God's worth?

Take a moment to read Psalm 136. Notice, *"His love endures forever!"* is stated twenty-six times. Have you truly grabbed onto that concept? Just in case, let me say it again ... his love DOES endure forever! And because of his great love, we have cause to worship and love him forever.

What are some ways you can actively "give thanks to him and praise his name?"

We respond actively in worship to who God is through our prayers to him, through reading his Word. We respond to God through singing and music, through building deeper relationships with others, through giving, serving, loving, sharing, and being obedient. We can worship God in every area of our lives.

> 1 Corinthians 10:31, *"So whether you eat or drink*
> *or whatever you do, do it all for the glory of God."*

What are some ways you could apply this in your own life and give thanks to him today?

God, who is so amazing, demands and deserves more than just a Sunday morning response to who he is. He is worthy of daily responses of worship from us. You might say, "how do I respond to God in worship everyday?" We have to remember - worship is an active response, a choice we make.

To continually be obedient to him, is to fix our minds on God and who he is every day. If we begin to lose sight of that, we must *"renew our minds"* and get our focus back on who God is.

What do you really love most?

Where do you need to grow?

What one step will you commit to over the next few weeks to grow toward living your life as a true worshiper of God?

Worship is about knowing and loving God
by Nelson Roth

Pam and I have had an awesome marriage. Though it was sometime ago, I remember very well how my heart was captured by her and we fell in love. I wanted to spend time with her. I was curious to learn more about her and all the things she liked. Although there have been challenging times over the years, *mostly due to my part* - we are more in love today than ever.

Relationship, like this, is something we can experience with another person. In a similar way, relationship like this is what God desires with each of us. The more we know him, the more we love him; and, the more we know and love God, the more we desire to give him what he desires and deserves - our worship.

How much does the worship of God and your relationship with God have a similar meaning for you?

In the previous Relevant Discipleship article, Jeff described worship in these words, *Worship is an active response to God in which we declare his worth!*

How much do you value relationship with God in your life?

The more we learn about God, we discover he actually pursues a relationship with us! God's primary desire is that we would know him; and then, seek a growing and loving relationship with him.

> John 3:16, *"For God so loved the world that he gave his one and only Son, that whoever believes in him shall not perish but have eternal life."*

> 1 John 3:16, *"This is how we know what love is: Jesus Christ laid down his life for us."*

How do you know him?

How are you moving forward in your knowledge of God and growing in your relationship with him?

John 17:3, *"Now this is eternal life: that they know you, the only true God, and Jesus Christ, whom you have sent."*

God's love for us is demonstrated in wanting a relationship with us before we ever want a relationship with him.

II Peter 3:9, *"The Lord is not slow in keeping his promise, as some understand slowness. Instead, he is patient with you, not wanting anyone to perish, but everyone to come to repentance."*

Romans 5:8, *"But God demonstrates his own love for us in this: While we were still sinners, Christ died for us."*

God gives each of us the choice whether we want to love him back or not. And, that's what makes worship genuine. Worship then, is the expression of voluntary love to God the Father for being loved so much by him.

This passage shows the difference in worship being a relationship above all of our religious activities. Matthew 15:7-9, *"You hypocrites! Isaiah was right when he prophesied about you: These people honor me with their lips, but their hearts are far from me. They worship me in vain; their teachings are merely human rules."*

When our relationship with God decreases, we seem to compensate by increasing our religious activity. Could it possibly be that religion, even though well intended, could be a major deterrent to truly worshiping God? More than any religious activity we could do, God's desire is a real and personal love relationship with him. This is why we worship him, because it is real and personal. In totality, worship is relational!

If worship is about knowing and loving God, what is going well for you and where are you challenged?

What will your next step be to practice the discipline of worship?

The weight of worship
by Brad Houchin

A few years ago, I took a class to learn the Hebrew alphabet and some basic root words. Understanding the Hebrew language created a whole new awareness while reading the Scriptures.

The teacher for the class shared an illustration that really impacted me. He pulled two large, weighty coins out of his pocket and put one in each of my hands. As I held these coins, he asked me to **lift up the one I believed to have the highest value.**

Thankfully, I made the right choice and lifted the heaviest one. The professor then began to explain to me what the word "kavod" meant. "Kavod" simply means heaviness or weighty; and when translated from the original Hebrew language, we get the word "glory."

Psalm 29:2 "Give unto the Lord the glory ("kavod") due unto his name; worship the Lord in the beauty of holiness."

So, I was correct when I held up the heavier coin because it had the greatest value. At the time, it was merely a guess; but, it made sense.

The definition of "glory" is not a picture of being burdened with a heavy load or exhausted from carrying a large weight, rather it is the picture of something that we lift up and respond to with the highest value over everything else.

Since the day I held those two coins and learned the meaning of the word "kavod," the word "glory" has taken on a deeper meaning for me.

As we write about worship being one of the 7 disciplines of a disciple, I want to bring "kavod" into our thinking. I believe it is vital for our worship to be on target, responding to God with our worship.

The "kavod" of God should be the motivating factor behind our every action.

Pause for a moment and make an honest reflection on what you hold up in highest value.

What place does God have in your life?

How do you picture your worship to God as a response to his "kavod"?

Luke 21:1-4 tells the story of the widow's offering, *"As Jesus looked up, he saw the rich putting their gifts into the temple treasury. He also saw a poor widow put in two very small copper coins. 'Truly I tell you,' he said, 'this poor widow has put in more than all the others. All these people gave their gifts out of their wealth; but she out of her poverty put in all she had to live on.'"*

How does the story of giving everything speak to you?

I believe too often it is easy to worship God when we are comfortable; just as it can be easy to give money out of our wealth.

There is a message for us to ponder in this story which I believe directly relates to worship and "kavod".

God is asking us to give our all in worship. Not just what we are comfortable giving him. He wants everything.

It is then, our worship to God becomes "kavod" (heavy, weighty); holding him up at the highest place. Not because we live a blessed and comfortable life. Not because we have a great worship band in our church or even a great church.

He wants our worship to be just like the widow who gave everything she had, because he is everything we need.

What is your take away from the idea of 'the weight of worship'?

Worship reveals Christ and my deep need of him

by Jeff Hegstrom

I love the words in the song, *When I Survey the Wondrous Cross.* The writer declares, *"Love so amazing, so divine, demands my soul, my life, my all."*

I want to be honest with you right now, there are times in my life when I go through the motions of worshiping God. Instead of trusting God completely, I unintentionally carry the burdens of life: relationships, finances, and schedules into my relationship with God. When my priorities are out of line, my worship to God becomes routine, without meaning; and, I walk away unamazed, discouraged and unchanged.

What is your experience when you just go through the motions of worship?

How do you overcome the feeling of apathy?

Recently, I read a quote that captured my attention about worship from Ben Patterson, campus pastor at Westmont College in Santa Barbara, California. Patterson said, *"Worship done as Jesus prescribed, in spirit and in truth, is an encounter, a meeting with the true and living God. You and I cannot come away from a meeting like that and remain the same."* When Christ is revealed in worship - as a true worshiper, I am changed!

Reading through the gospels, I have found endless accounts of how Jesus spent time with people, loving them, healing them, teaching them, walking and living his life with and among them. The incredible thing is as you read each of these encounters, Jesus' true identity was revealed and people's lives were changed forever.

In the gospel written by Luke, chapter 5:3-8, Jesus was by the lake teaching when he saw two fishermen washing their nets. The Bible says:

"He got into one of the boats, the one belonging to Simon, and asked him to put out a little from the shore. Then he sat down and taught the people from the boat. When he had finished speaking, he said to Simon, "Put out into deep water, and let down the nets for a catch." Simon answered, "Master, we've worked hard all night and haven't caught anything. But because you say so, I will let down the nets." When they had done so, they caught such a large number of fish that their nets began to break. So they signaled their partners in the other boat to come and help them, and they came and filled both boats so full that they began to sink. When Simon Peter saw this, he fell at Jesus' knees and said, "Go away from me, Lord; I am a sinful man!"

As you can see, when we come to Jesus in our everyday life, and live out our lives before him in authentic worship (in spirit and truth), not only is the glory of God revealed in us through the gift of his Son Jesus Christ; but, his amazing love reveals our deepest and greatest need ... our need for more of him!

A love that is amazing demands my response.

Look at how Peter, James and John responded to being in the presence of Jesus in verse 11, *"So they pulled their boats up on shore, left everything and followed him."*

Being in the revealing presence and the glory of Jesus Christ changed everything! Their lives were transformed. They bowed down in worship, surrendered everything and followed Jesus!

How are you letting Jesus be revealed in your everyday life?

How are you allowing your life to be changed as you worship in his presence?

Read Romans 12:1 and as you reflect, how can you respond today to live out a life of worship by Christ being revealed through you?

A disciple maker who is relevant prays
by Jeff Hegstrom

Prayer is a mark of spiritual health. For the Christian, prayer is like breathing. Prayer is essential for spiritual health, just like breathing is essential for our physical well-being. God's Word instructs believers in Philippians 4:6-7 to pray *"in every situation."*

What does prayer mean to you?   **How is prayer like breathing?**

Prayer is the communication of the soul with the Spirit of the living God.

Following Jesus' example, we spend time alone in prayer. Mark 1:35, *"Very early in the morning, while it was still dark, Jesus got up, left the house and went off to a solitary place, where he prayed."*

And, we also pray together with others. Matthew 18:20, *"...For where two or three gather in my name, there am I with them."* Both experiences connect us to him.

In the book of Acts, we see the early church praying. Groups of believers gathered and prayed and experienced the presence, peace, and power of Christ.

How is prayer a part of your small group or when you gather with others?

How open and honest are the members in your group? How often do they pray about what really matters?

How does your small group experience the presence, peace and power of Christ when they gather?

Let's take a closer look at the role of prayer and the impact on the early church. As you spend time in the book of Acts, take time to think through how the church grew and experienced the presence, peace and power of Christ through prayer.

Prayer was vital for the early church. It was a relational experience both with God and others.

The early church was born out of a prayer meeting of 120 people - Acts 1:14, *"they all joined together constantly in prayer."*

Members of the early church prayed when they got together - Acts 2:42, *"they devoted themselves ... to the fellowship ... and to prayer."*

As these early believers lived life together and grew in relationship they responded to every situation out of this new lifestyle of prayer.

1. When they needed guidance - Acts 1:24, *"Then they prayed, Lord you know everyone's heart. Show us which of these two you have chosen."*
2. Being responsible leaders - Acts 6:4, *"and will give our attention to prayer and the ministry of the Word."*
3. When commissioning people for service - Acts 6:6, *"They presented these men to the apostles, who prayed and laid their hands on them."*
4. When they faced death - Acts 7:59-60, *"While they were stoning him, Stephen prayed."*
5. When they were burdened for others' spiritual needs - Acts 8:15, *"When they arrived, they prayed for them that they might receive the Holy Spirit."*
6. When ministering to the sick and hopeless - Acts 9:40, *"Peter got down on his knees and prayed. Turning toward the dead woman, he said, Tabitha, get up."*
7. When they were challenged by opposition and danger - Acts 12:5, *"Peter was kept in prison, but the church was earnestly praying."*
8. When leaving from one place to another - Acts 21:5, *"All of the disciples and their wives and children accompanied us out of the city, and there on the beach we knelt to pray."*

Prayer was like breathing for the early church, it was essential. Prayer was part of their relationship with God and each other. Prayer brought confidence and guidance for all of their responses. And with prayer, Christ was revealed. Through communion with the Spirit they had so much more than some distant connection.

What has the Holy Spirit revealed to you about prayer?

How will you apply what the Holy Spirit has shown you about prayer?

How will you know when you have experienced prayer like this?

Prayer and relationship
by Nelson Roth

As a young pastor, my prayer life began to change in significant ways in the early 1980's when Peter Lord, my mentor at the time, said to me, "God is not only the most high God, he is also the most nigh God!" His statement caused an important shift for me from saying prayers to a distant Creator to having conversations with my loving Heavenly Father.

Prayer that is relevant is relational! Jesus and Paul reinforce Peter Lord's words when they say in scriptures to pray to your Father. Jesus in Matthew 6:9 says, *"This, then, is how you should pray: Our Father in heaven..."* Paul says, *"I bow my knees before the Father"* in Ephesians 3:14.

"What father among you, if his son asks for a fish, will instead of a fish give him a serpent?" Jesus speaks these words in Luke 11:11 expressing the intimate, loving relationship believers can experience with Father God, their Daddy. It is the same as the healthy, loving relationships we have with our biological fathers.

What are your thoughts about the most high God and most nigh God?

What would a self evaluation of your prayer life based on a personal relationship with God look like?

J.I. Packer wrote a great book titled, *Knowing God*. At one point in the book, he asks an important question: *Do we desire such knowledge of God? Then, first, we must recognize how much we lack knowledge of God. We must learn to measure ourselves, not by our knowledge about God, not by our gifts and responsibilities in the church, but by how we pray and what goes on in our hearts. Many of us, I suspect, have no idea how impoverished we are at this level. Let us ask the Lord to show us.*

Packer's words about our *lack of knowing God and being impoverished* is a reminder to me of another impactful conversation with Peter Lord, when he said, "Knowing and loving God go together. The more you love him, the more you will want to know him and the more that you know him the more you will love him."

How is prayer relational for you?

According to the J.I. Packer statement, we need to evaluate our relationship with God and our knowledge of God: We must learn to measure ourselves by how we pray and what goes on in our hearts.

How are you impacted with the idea about prayer being relational?

In the matter of knowing and loving God, where would you start for continued growth in your life?

Knowing God is more than knowing about him; it is a matter of dealing with him as he opens up to you, and being dealt with by him as he takes knowledge of you.
J.I. Packer

Praying in response to the promises of God
by Brad Houchin

After Hurricane Katrina, the Relevant Ministry team 'lived life on mission,' by coming alongside families whose homes were affected by the storm. During that time, we had the privilege to hear many of their life stories through this serving ministry. Often, these opportunities opened the door for ministry through prayer. Never can I remember a time when someone turned down the offer for us to pray with them.

There will always be times in which we need to stop what we are doing immediately, and pray. These times may be from an unexpected phone call regarding a loved one being rushed to the hospital, a disaster just struck somewhere in the world or you're running late for an important meeting and you are stuck in traffic. The list can go on and on. Often in these times, one of our first reactions is to pray, "Heavenly Father, I need your help!"

There is something about prayer, even for those who do not have an intimate relationship with God. It makes sense to pray or at least receive prayer in times of crisis and need. But as children of God, prayer should be much more than crying out of a feeling of hopelessness.

Our prayer, even in times of crisis and need, should be in response to the promises of God.

"How great is the love the Father has lavished on us, that we should be called children of God! And that is what we are! The reason the world does not know us is that it did not know him."
1 John 3:1

How does knowing you are a child of God give you more confidence to pray?

What do you believe about boldly approaching God with your prayer requests?

Hebrews 4:14-16, *"Therefore, since we have a great high priest who has gone through the heavens, Jesus the Son of God, let us hold firmly to the faith we profess. For we do not have a high priest who is unable to sympathize with our weaknesses, but we have one who has been tempted in every way, just as we are – yet was without sin. So let us come boldly to the throne of our gracious God. There we will receive his mercy, and we will find grace to help us when we need it most."*

Being a child of God gives us direct access to his throne. We can trust our Heavenly Father hears our prayers and his grace will be sufficient for our needs.

How does this confidence encourage your prayer to be a response to him rather than a reaction to a circumstance?

1 John 5:1-5, *"Everyone who believes that Jesus is the Christ is born of God, and everyone who loves the father loves his child as well. This is how we know that we love the children of God: by loving God and carrying out his commands. In fact, this is love for God: to keep his commands. And his commands are not burdensome, for everyone born of God overcomes the world. This is the victory that has overcome the world, even our faith. Who is it that overcomes the world? Only the one who believes that Jesus is the Son of God."*

Prayer becomes responsive when we understand the promise that we have already overcome the trials and temptations of this world. Through our belief in Jesus Christ, our requests should be prayed in confidence because we trust his will in his way.

Hebrews 4:13, *"Nothing in all creation is hidden from God's sight. Everything is uncovered and laid bare before the eyes of him to whom we must give account."*

He already knows every need, how will you respond in prayer today?

In prayer Christ is revealed to us
by Nelson Roth

Like the seasons of the year, prayer seems to have cycles. Each season of prayer has purpose just like the seasons of the year; and each a contributing part to God unveiling answers to questions we may have about the future. The unveiling is that incredible season when Christ pulls back the curtain revealing his plans and ways as we pray.

In prayer, Christ is revealed to us.

Our prayer experience may not always be a revelation though, and that's why we're encouraged to persevere in our prayers. Luke 18:1, *"always pray and not give up."*

When we persevere, here's some promises of Christ revealing his ways at the right time.

- Jeremiah 33:3, *"call to me and I will answer you"*

- John 14:13, *"I will do whatever you ask in my name"*

- James 5:16, *"the prayer of a righteous man is powerful and effective"*

- Ephesians 3:20, *"do immeasurably more than all we ask or imagine"*

Has there been a time for you when questions about your future were unanswered? Imagine what it must have been like for John when he was alone and rejected on the Isle of Patmos. From the scriptures, we learn Christ was revealed to John, along with the incredible message about the future. It's recorded in the book of Revelation, which by the way means unveiling! Here's where Christ first came to John:

> Revelation 1:12-13, 17, *"I turned around to see the voice that was speaking to me. And when I turned I saw seven golden lampstands, and among the lampstands was someone like a son of man, dressed in a robe reaching down to his feet and with a golden sash around his chest. ... When I saw him, I fell at his feet as though dead. Then he placed his right hand on me and said: Do not be afraid. I am the First and the Last. I am the Living One; I was dead, and now look, I am alive for ever and ever!"*

And then Christ began to lay out the future, by telling John, *"Write, therefore, what you have seen, what is now and what will take place later."* Revelation 1:19

Christ revealing the future is dependent upon God's timing of course; but, are there things we can do to hinder our prayers and Christ being revealed?

These verses tell us we can hinder revelation that God is wanting to give to us.

- Psalm 66:18, "If I had cherished sin in my heart, the Lord would not have listened"

- James 4:2-3, "you ask with wrong motives"

- James 1:5-7, "when he asks, he must believe and not doubt"

What might God be saying to you around the verses above?

In prayer, Christ is revealed to us. How might you answer the following questions?

If prayer had seasons, what season are you currently experiencing?

How might you be hindering Christ being revealed in your prayer life?

What promises from the scriptures are increasing your faith?

God's Word, foundational for life
by Nelson Roth

"And we also thank God continually because, when you received the word of God, which you heard from us, you accepted it not as the word of men, but as it actually is, the word of God, which is at work in you who believe."
1 Thessalonians 2:13

The Bible is God's written word to us. *"All Scripture is God-breathed and is useful for teaching, rebuking, correcting and training in righteousness, so that the man of God may be thoroughly equipped for every good work."* 2 Timothy 3:16-17

In what ways do you currently practice the spiritual discipline of Bible reading and study?

The impact of the Word was foundational in the lives of the first century believers and was vital for spiritual health and growth. The Word that they experienced was both the written Word of God, the scriptures; and, the Word proclaimed that aligned with scriptures.

"But the word of God continued to increase and spread."
Acts 12:24

"In this way the word of the Lord spread widely and grew in power."
Acts 19:20

How has the spiritual discipline of Bible study impacted your life?

Such impact is possible because of these four realities about the Word of God ... it's true - alive - absolute - and powerful.

God's Word is true:
"...sanctify them by the truth, your word is truth." John 17:17

God's Word is alive:
"...the word of the Lord endureth forever." 1 Peter 1:25
"...heaven and earth shall pass away but my words shall not pass away." Matthew 24:35
"...being born again not of corruptible seed, but of incorruptible, by the word of God, which liveth and abideth forever." 1 Peter 1:23

God's Word is absolute:
"As for God, his way is perfect; the word of the Lord is flawless." Psalm 18:30

God's Word is powerful:
"For the word of God is living and active. Sharper than any double-edged sword, it penetrates even to dividing soul and spirit, joints and marrow; it judges the thoughts and attitudes of the heart." Hebrews 4:12

How do each of these four realities align with your current personal beliefs?

God's Word is: true – alive – absolute – and powerful; and it teaches us that:

1. **God desires to reveal himself to us.** Romans 1:19-20, *"Since what may be known about God is plain to them, because God has made it plain to them. For since the creation of the world God's invisible qualities - his eternal power and divine nature - have been clearly seen, being understood from what has been made, so that men are without excuse."*

2. **Though we are out of relationship with God and separated from him by sin, he loves us.** Romans 6:23, *"For the wages of sin is death, but the gift of God is eternal life in Christ Jesus our Lord."*

3. **There is hope if we make the right response to God's love demonstrated in his gift of Jesus Christ.** Romans 5:15, 18, *"...how much more did God's grace and the gift that came by the grace of the one man, Jesus Christ, overflow to the many!... just as the result of one trespass was condemnation for all men, so also the result of the act of righteousness was justification that brings life for all men."*

Romans 10:13, *"For everyone who calls on the name of the Lord will be saved."*

What is your personal relationship with the author of the Bible?

God's Word is your foundation for life. In the Bible, we have trustworthy authority for faith and life.

How have you been challenged about the Word being foundational for your life?

What would look different about your life with God's Word as the foundation?

What is one specific step that you can take today to make God's Word the foundation for your life?

God relates to us through his Word
by Jeff Hegstrom

God's Word teaches us that *relationships matter*. From the beginning of Genesis, we not only see the relationship of the Trinity (the Father, Son and Holy Spirit); but, we also see God's love relationship with his creation as he walked daily in fellowship with Adam and Eve in the garden. (Genesis 2:8)

The Gospel of John clearly declares God's love for mankind. The scripture also affirms just how much our **relationship with him matters.** John 1:14 tells us, *"The Word became flesh and dwelt among us."* God loves us so much that he sent his one and only Son into the world to live among us, to have relationship and fellowship with mankind that the world may truly know him and be saved. (John 3:16-18)

If I asked, "How do you have an ongoing relationship with God?" Many of you might say, through spending time in prayer and reading God's Word. These are incredible answers; but, how often do you actually take the time to invest in your relationship with God through prayer and reading?

How would you evaluate your relationship with God and his Word?

Never · · · · · · · · Casual · · · · · · · · Somewhat steady · · · · · · · · Reliant upon God

How often do you take the time to stop and listen to God speak to you through his Word?

God is relational, and he relates to us through his Word.
The Bible isn't just a good read, a history book, or a book of rules and regulations. The Bible is God's very words, written to us to declare his love and offer hope and salvation for all who will believe. He is the author and we are the recipients of his love story that he has written for us and is writing in us. God has given us his word through the Bible that we may truly know him and his great love for us. From the Bible, we learn how to live the life God fully intends for us to live through an authentic relationship with him.

God's Word is INTERACTIVE
Psalm 119:105, *"Thy word is a lamp unto my feet and a light unto my path."*
Isaiah 55:11, *"So is my word that goes out from my mouth: It will not return to me empty, but will accomplish what I desire and achieve the purpose for which I sent it."*

God's Word is INSTRUCTIVE
Timothy 3:16-17, *"All Scripture is God breathed and is useful for teaching, rebuking, correcting and training in righteousness, so that the man of God may be thoroughly equipped for every good work."*

Romans 15:4, *"For everything that was written in the past was written to teach us, so that through endurance and the encouragement of the Scriptures we might have hope."*

God's Word is INTIMATE

Romans 10:8, *"...The word is near you; it is in your mouth and in your heart."*

Psalm 119:9-16, *"How can a young man keep his way pure? By living according to your word. I seek you with all my heart; do not let me stray from your commands. I have hidden your word in my heart that I might not sin against you...I meditate on your precepts and consider your ways. I delight in your decrees; I will not neglect your word."*

I remember when I was serving as a Student Ministries Pastor. There was a young lady in high school who fell in love with God and his Word. She came to me one Sunday morning to ask if she could share something about God's Word with the other students in our youth service. That morning, she got up in front of all of her peers, and said she had been reading in the book of Psalms. She couldn't believe something written so long ago applied exactly to her life and what she was going through at that very moment. She proceeded to share how God knows exactly what you need and what you are going through; and, if you will read his Word, his love letter to you, he will use his Word to speak directly to you and your circumstances.

What a powerful revelation and testimony about the relationship of God's Word in your life straight from the heart of a teenager. I love what the Psalmist said about God's Word ... *"The law of the Lord is perfect, reviving the soul. The statutes of the Lord are trustworthy, making wise the simple. The precepts of the Lord are right, giving joy to the heart. The commands of the Lord are radiant, giving light to the eyes. The fear of the Lord is pure, enduring forever. The ordinances of the Lord are sure and altogether righteous. They are more precious than gold, than much pure gold; they are sweeter than honey, than honey from the comb. By them is your servant warned; in keeping them there is great reward."* Psalm 19:7-11

When is the last time God spoke directly to you about your circumstances through his Word? How did that impact you?

How could you begin to intentionally invest in your relationship with God through his Word?

What difference do you believe it would make in your life?

What difference do you believe it would make in your relationship with God?

WORD

If I pay attention to a little word
by Brad Houchin

The word "if," as small as it is, can have a great effect on us. Sometimes that effect can be a good thing, other times not so good. The word "if" could just be the most important word of our lives. Think about it this way...

> ... if I do not cook this long enough, I could get sick
> ... if I do not make my mortgage payment, I will lose my house.
> ... if I do not show up to work each day, I will lose my job.
> ... if it does not rain soon, the farmers will lose their crops.
> ... if I do not come up for air, I will drown.
> ... if she......., then I will.....
> ... if he would only....., then I would

The list of "if'" statements can go on and on.

How can this little word, "if," be more important than God, Jesus, the Bible and love? Well, I am not saying it is; however, I do believe without the word "if" the words listed above are mere words to us.

"If" most often requires an action or response.

> James 2:14-19, *"What good is it, dear brothers and sisters, **if** you say you have faith but don't show it by your actions? Can that kind of faith save anyone? Suppose you see a brother or sister who has no food or clothing, and you say, 'Good-bye and have a good day; stay warm and eat well' — but then you don't give that person any food or clothing. What good does that do? So you see, faith by itself isn't enough. Unless it produces good deeds, it is dead and useless...'How can you show me your faith **if** you don't have good deeds? I will show you my faith by my good deeds.'"*

How important is the word "if" in this passage of James?

The Bible tells us even the demons believe in God. It is the "if" which makes the difference in our belief of God.

> Romans 10:9, *"**If** you confess with your mouth, 'Jesus is Lord', and believe in your heart God raised him from the dead, you will be saved."*

What is God's promised response to us if we do the "if" of this passage?

2 Chronicles 7:14, *"If my people, who are called by my name, will humble themselves and pray and seek my face and turn from their wicked ways, then I will hear from heaven, and I will forgive their sin and heal their land."*

Pause for a moment and reflect on the great promise in this passage of scripture. I would even encourage you to respond to this passage with prayer.

What is God's promised response to us if we do the "if" of this passage?

A mark of spiritual healthiness is being committed to God's word, the Bible! This commitment is more than reading and studying, it is paying attention to the "ifs" and doing them.

James 1:22-25, *"Do not merely listen to the word, and so deceive yourselves. Do what it says. Anyone who listens to the word but does not do what it says is like someone who looks at his face in a mirror and, after looking at himself, goes away and immediately forgets what he looks like. But whoever looks intently into the perfect law that gives freedom, and continues in it—not forgetting what they have heard, but doing it—they will be blessed in what they do."*

Spend some time looking up the following passages of scripture. What are the "ifs" and what are the responses God promises?

Colossians 1:21-23

Isaiah 40:31

Matthew 11:28-29

Proverbs 1:33

Proverbs 3:5-6

1 Peter 5:6-10

The word "if" has so much power throughout the Bible!

When we respond to God with the "if" he asks of us, how does he promise to respond to us?

How does knowing that, make it all worth doing the "if"?

In the Word is a word for you
by Nelson Roth

God reveals himself through his Word! So, in the Word, there's a word for you. Because God wants each of us to know him and the plans that he has for us he reveals himself to us in various ways. Psalm 19:7-8, *"The law of the Lord is perfect, reviving the soul; the testimony of the Lord is sure, making wise the simple; the precepts of the Lord are right, rejoicing the heart; the commandment of the Lord is pure, enlightening the eyes."*

How might God be revealing himself, or saying something in particular to you today?

A young man in his mid-twenties purchased a book at the airport newsstand to read during a long flight he was about to take. When he was seated, he found himself next to a lady about his age. Each greeted the other and then the young man began to read his new book. After a half- hour or so, he put the book down not being able to really get into it. He then struck up a conversation with the young lady. She was very interesting and they found that they had a number of things in common. The conversation was so energizing that the couple continued to talk the rest of the flight. As the plane landed they exchanged names and contact information. It was at that moment that the young man realized that the lady was the author of his new book. Wow, what a surprise! That night in his hotel room the young man decided to pick up the book to try to read it again. This time he was not able to put it down. He kept on reading through the night. What was the difference? He knew and had fallen in love with the author!

How does this story impact you?

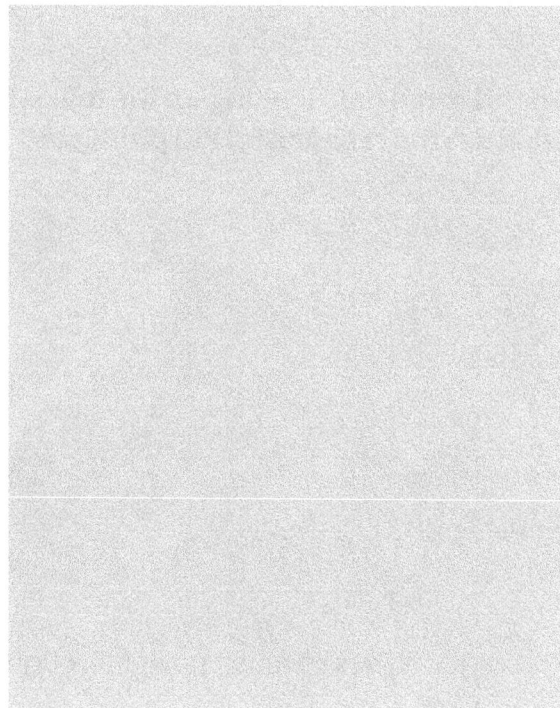

God's desire is to reveal himself to us!

In the Psalm 19 passage, mentioned in the beginning of this article, it speaks of two kinds of revelation, both general and special. General revelation and special revelation are two theological references about how God reveals himself.

General revelation refers to God revealing himself through nature and his creation. The Bible tells us this in verse one of Psalm 19, *"The heavens declare the glory of God; the skies proclaim the work of his hands."*

Special revelation is called special because God at certain times throughout history has chosen to reveal himself by miraculous or supernatural means.

God, by preserving his Word for us and making himself known to the readers of the Word, is the most commonly shared form of special revelation. Psalm 19:8 refers to it as *"enlightening the eyes."*

Here is a New Testament example of special revelation. Luke 2:10-11, *"And the angel said to them, "Fear not, for behold, I bring you good news of great joy that will be for all the people. For unto you is born this day in the city of David a Savior, who is Christ the Lord."*

God supernaturally gifted the writers of Scripture to accurately record his message through each author's personality and style. 2 Peter 1:21, *"For the prophecy came not in old time by the will of man: but holy men of God spake as they were moved by the Holy Ghost."* 2 Timothy 3:16-17, *"All Scripture is breathed out by God and profitable for teaching, for reproof, for correction, and for training in righteousness, that the man of God may be complete, equipped for every good work."* God reveals himself and he does it through his Word in both general and specific ways.

What does it do to you when you look to the heavens that declare the glory of God or as you notice the skies that proclaim the work of his hands?

What is the word he has for you in his Word?

What can you do to fall in love with the author of the Word?

Ministry and ministers
by Nelson Roth

Let's consider the following three questions: Who are the ministers? What is ministry? Why is ministry important?

First: Who are the ministers?
1 Corinthians 3:6-9 reads, *"I planted the seed, Apollos watered it, but God made it grow...For we are God's fellow workers..."* This verse speaks of the inclusiveness of ministry. The verse also tells us **ministry is relational. It connects with others, and it works along with others.**

Ministry in our day has often taken on more of a vocational meaning; as we look to pastors and clergy to be the ministers. Clergy do spend their life in the ministry and they are rightly designated as ministers; but, they are not the only ones who can be or are to be involved in ministry.

In the local church, there is an absolute indispensability of each and every believer exercising their ministry gifts and abilities. The dynamic ministry of the early church came from gifted leaders building up the saints - helping them discover and develop spiritual gifts and releasing them into ministry.

Local church leaders are to, *"equip God's people for works of service, so that the body of Christ may be built up."* Ephesians 4:12.

What challenges might exist because of preconceived ideas about the roles of clergy and laity?

The equipped members of the local church then are to also do ministry. Ephesians 4:16, *"From him the whole body, joined and held together by every supporting ligament, grows and builds itself up in love, as each part does its work."*

What has been your past ministry experience?

What are your spiritual gifts?

What spiritual gifts have others noticed in you?

Question two: What is ministry?
The word ministry is from the Greek word *diakoneo*, meaning "to serve" or *douleuo*, meaning "to serve as a slave." In the New Testament, ministry is seen as service to God and to other people in his name. Jesus provided the pattern for Christian ministry.

Matthew 20:28, *"the Son of Man did not come to be served, but to serve, and to give his life as a ransom for many."*

John 13:14-15, *"Now that I, your Lord and Teacher, have washed your feet, you also should wash one another's feet. I have set you an example that you should do as I have done for you."*

Ministry is serving God by serving others with the spiritual gifts and abilities he has given.

Ministry is about doing what we are able to do with God's help. **Ministry is about responding to needs that we see.** Ministry is not about being busy; rather, it is more about being willing to do the right things at the right time. It's about knowing God's will and agreeing with him when we recognize his activity. Ministry is helping to meet genuine needs and responding in Jesus' name, sharing the good news of the gospel.

The third question: Why is ministry important?
Implementing ministry into your life means taking steps to begin serving like Jesus served. **And, ministry that is relevant reveals Christ.** Serving like Jesus served, means being available. *"Two blind men...shouted, 'Lord, have mercy on us!'...Jesus stopped and called them. 'What do you want me to do for you?' he asked."* Matthew. 20:30-32

What is the important thing you see Jesus doing here?

To serve like Jesus served, I must be willing to be available, which might also mean being interrupted. Proverbs 3:28, *"Do not say to your neighbor, 'Come back later; I'll give it tomorrow' - when you now have it with you."*

In Luke 10:30-37, Jesus tells the parable of The Good Samaritan; and in it we see three different responses toward the person who was in need of help.
- One kept his distance.
- Another was curious, but did not get involved.
- The Samaritan not only saw the need, but he responded to the man in need.

How would you evaluate your ministry related to its role in carrying out the Great Commission?

Ministry that is relevant is believers serving others in Jesus' name, doing good deeds and sharing the Good News.

MINISTRY

Healthy ministry begins with relationship
by Jeff Hegstrom

When I first started out in ministry, I willingly admit I knew absolutely nothing, but I had a passion to "do" something for God. I wanted to make a difference! I longed for God to use the good and bad experiences I had in my life and I wanted to share my spiritual life journey to bring hope to the hopeless and win the lost for him.

I still love that kind of raw passion for God; but, what I didn't understand back then was I couldn't do it alone. During the first three years of ministry, I almost burned myself out trying to "do" everything and reach out to every age group. I had this misguided idea that as a paid staff member, I should and could meet all the needs of the ministry.

One evening, as I was getting ready to kick off one of our weekly ministries to college students, I broke. Wow, that's an honest thought. I broke ... I broke, and I couldn't fix me, so right then and there I cried out to God for help and he answered me (Psalm 40:1-3) and showed me that I was trying to serve him, without him.

My priorities were completely out of line and as a result I had nothing left to give. I was spent. You see, God didn't call believers to "do" ministry for him. He first called us to "be" in him.

In John 15:7-8, Jesus teaches us that it is out of our relationship and connectedness with him that we will bear much fruit and show ourselves to be his disciple.

Ministry that is relevant ... begins with an authentic relationship with God through Jesus Christ.

Ministry begins with being found in Christ, learning to hear his voice, seeking to know his heart, and following after his will. When we place our relationship with Christ above everything else in this life, the product will not be your exhausted efforts of "doing" ministry; but ministry will come from the inside out, and your life will "bear much fruit!"

Ministry that is relevant ... happens when we are in relationship with others.

As a leader, I am constantly challenged by the Holy Spirit to live out Ephesians 4:11-16. God didn't call you or me to be the lone ranger in our ministries, but *"to prepare God's people for works of service so that the body of Christ may be built up."* The role of healthy leadership is to equip and empower the whole body of Christ to become all that God has called his church to be. God has greatly gifted the whole body of Christ to serve together; everyone according to their gifts, and what you must understand is that includes you. God has given you a spiritual gift(s) that is special and specific for you to use to minister and build up the body of Christ, his church; and every part is needed for the church to grow strong and healthy. When you are using your spiritual gifts and ministering in your relationship with others, you will not only find yourself growing healthy; but the church begins to grow healthy too.

What is your spiritual gift(s)?

How are you using your spiritual gifts to build up the body of Christ?

If not, what is keeping you from your vital role in the body of Christ?

Stop and ask God to help you grow closer in your RELATIONSHIP with him. Then, ask him to help you discover your spiritual gifts and where you can use your gifts in RELATIONSHIP with others.

I know sometimes life's demands get overwhelming. It's so easy to lose focus on what really matters and begin "doing" ministry. Let me encourage you to resist the temptation to "do" ministry alone and in your own strength. When we have our priorities set on our relationship with Christ and then others; God can produce in us a healthy, growing life and ministry that bears much fruit; proving you are his disciple!

MINISTRY

Gifted to glorify God
by Brad Houchin

My wife and I have been serving in church ministry for over two decades now. Our introduction to ministry began as volunteers with a youth ministry. We had two roles, crowd control and helping with events. Over time, the responsibilities began to change along with our hearts. We grew in confidence and began to say, "yes" to more and more opportunities; eventually, leading to a full-time position as a student pastor.

We have always loved hanging out with students; but reflecting back over the years, becoming a "student pastor" never was the goal. In fact, right after our first son was born; my wife and I had both made the decision to take time for family and to take a break from student ministry. We had just landed at a new church home and the time to make this ministry break was available for us. Well...less than ten months later we were leading student ministries again; and in 2004, we left a job of twelve years and took a full-time position as Director of Student Ministries at a church in Central Illinois. God had instilled in us a passion for young people and we could not say, "no" to serving.

What about you? What are you really passionate about? How are you choosing to respond relevantly?

If you are a follower of Christ, then God has uniquely gifted you for ministry and he has surrounded you with ministry opportunities to use those gifts. The challenge is overwhelming and the many reasons we can come up with to not serve can be....

- I am too busy with work
- I don't know what to say to people
- I don't do youth (I ran across this many times searching for volunteers)
- I don't want to miss church services
- I don't know the Bible well enough
- I have too much of a past

We can miss opportunities to use our gifts for numerous reasons; but, what we need to understand is the opportunity in front of each of us is twofold. It is about God impacting others through you, and also about you simply saying, "yes."

Ministry that is relevant is responsive... for the purpose of bringing glory to God.

1 Peter 4:10-11, *"Each of you should use whatever gift you have received to serve others, as faithful stewards of God's grace in its various forms. If anyone speaks, they should do so as one who speaks the very words of God. If anyone serves, they should do so with the strength God provides, so that in all things God may be praised through Jesus Christ. To him be the glory and the power for ever and ever. Amen."*

If God has given you gifts, personality, and passion; then he will lead and guide you along the path with opportunities to glorify him.

Philippians 2:13, *"For it is God who works in you to will and to act according to his good purpose."*

The turning point in our relationship is when we realize we have received gifts from God; but, we can't carry out the work he has for us without him. God wants to come alongside us and help us to obey him and then he gives us the power to do what he wants. We then need to respond to God and submit to his control and let him work in our lives.

At the point my wife and I chose to say "yes" to working with the youth full-time, we said "yes" to obedience and the calling he had for us. We have not turned back. Our journey has been an experience with God we would not have traded for the "plans" we had for our lives. He has led us each step of the way and has allowed us the privilege to be used for his glory.

"Whatever you do, do it all for the glory of God" - 1 Corinthians 10:31b

Maybe it isn't a full-time ministry position for you, but what is God asking of you?

What area can God be glorified through in your life?

How can hearts be reached by your response of obedience to God?

After spending some time with God, what has he placed in your heart?

MINISTRY

What do clay pots have to do with ministry?
by Nelson Roth

In 2 Corinthians chapter four, Paul explains what Christian ministry is all about.

The word for ministry he uses in verse one means, *giving service to another with the idea that this service is being done because of the command of someone superior to you.* So, Paul says it correctly when in verse five he says, *"...we don't preach ourselves, but Christ as Lord, and ourselves as servants."*

How does the idea of being a servant and serving in this way settle with you?

Paul explains ministry further with the picture of a clay pot in verse seven. When it comes to clay pots they can serve two purposes, to either be on display or to be functional because of the contents they carry inside.

Where do you think Paul is headed with this illustration?

What point do you think he wants to make?

In verse six, he says that the content of a Christian's clay pot is, *"...his light shining in our hearts."* Verse seven, *"...we have this treasure in jars of clay."*

How does being either a clay pot on display or being a functional pot challenge you?

Paul now answers the question of what clay pots have to do with ministry. In verse ten, he says, *"...that the life of Jesus may also be revealed in our body."*

Next, he gives us three final points of encouragement for how Christ can be revealed through our lives in our ministry.

1. There will be difficult times, but we choose whether to react or respond. Most reactions are knee-jerk and negative. Responses are intentional steps in the right direction.

    "We are hard pressed on every side, but not crushed;
    perplexed, but not in despair; persecuted, but not abandoned; struck
    down, but not destroyed." (vs. 8-9)

2. Some functional clay pots are broken to release their valuable contents. When this happens, we recognize where our strength comes from. In being broken, we rely on Christ; he shines and is revealed in even greater ways.

    "Therefore we do not lose heart. Though outwardly we are wasting away,
    yet inwardly we are being renewed day by day." (vs. 16)

3. Our understanding of and vision for the future becomes crystal clear and we discover purpose in living life on mission.

    "So we fix our eyes not on what is seen, but on what is unseen, since what is
    seen is temporary, but what is unseen is eternal." (vs. 18)

How is God speaking to you about serving and ministry?

Which of Paul's final three points is the most challenging for you?

What can you take away from the challenge of being a clay pot revealing Christ?

Copyright © Relevant Ministry, Inc.

43

DISCIPLESHIP
growing Godly in character with a foundation of personal values and purpose

Becoming faithful learners and followers of Jesus Christ
by Jeff Hegstrom

What is discipleship?
It's an organic process where believers implement a healthy biblical foundation within their lives. The process brings about transformational growth and movement from spiritual infancy, to spiritual adolescence, and on to spiritual maturity ... it's becoming more like the Lord Jesus Christ.

Jesus' example of discipleship:
Throughout the gospels, Jesus models what true discipleship looks like. From his invitation to the disciples to *leave everything behind and follow him, to the way he personally walked and lived out his life.* With his disciples he taught, modeled, challenged, corrected, revealed, comforted, and empowered. **Jesus invited his disciples to be with him in every circumstance of life, to be transformed in personal character in order to be like him.** Transformation is at the heart of biblical discipleship.

What do you think is the outcome of true biblical discipleship?

A biblical disciple is a "learner and follower" of Jesus Christ.

Following Jesus means being in relationship with him and wholeheartedly serving him while traveling life's journey.

Discipleship is all about learning from and living out life in the ways of Jesus.

> John 13:13-15, *"You call me 'Teacher' and 'Lord,' and you are right, because that's what I am. And since I, your Lord and Teacher, have washed your feet, you ought to wash each other's feet. I have given you an example to follow. Do as I have done to you."*

> 1 Peter 2:21, *"To this you were called, because Christ suffered for you, leaving you an example, that you should follow in his steps."*

The goal of discipleship is becoming more like Jesus.

> Luke 6:40, *"A student is not above his teacher, but everyone who is fully trained will be like his teacher."*

Here are four responsibilities as a growing disciple of Jesus Christ:

Live out the Greatest Commandment
Matthew 22:36-39, *"Teacher, which is the greatest commandment in the Law?" Jesus replied: " 'Love the Lord your God with all your heart and with all your soul and with all your mind.' This is the first and greatest commandment. And the second is like it: 'Love your neighbor as yourself.'*

Yield to a life surrendered and centered in Christ
Matthew 16:24, *"Then Jesus said to his disciples, "If anyone would come after me, he must deny himself and take up his cross and follow me."*

Be obedient to the Word of God
To the Jews who had believed him, Jesus said in John 8:31, *"If you hold to my teaching, you are really my disciples."* John 10:27, *"My sheep listen to my voice; I know them, and they follow me."*

Respond to the Great Commission
Jesus teaches us that as his disciples ... you and I are also called to be disciple makers. Jesus wants every believer to intentionally share what he/she is learning from him. Who has God placed in your life that may want to know more about him and follow him?

As the Master Teacher, Jesus calls his disciples (every believer) in Matthew 28:19-20 to *"Go into all the world and make disciples of every nation, baptizing them in the name of the Father and of the Son and of the Holy Spirit, and teaching them to obey everything I have commanded you. And surely I am with you always, to the very end of the age."*

What is one area out of the four responsibilities of a growing disciple that you would like to develop?

What is God's role/your role in the life of a growing disciple?

Taking it to the next level: Currently, how do you relate to these four stages of growth as a disciple? Circle one of the four stages that best describe you on this organic process of biblical discipleship.

Infant · · · · · · · · Child · · · · · · · · Adolescent · · · · · · · · Mature

Why did you choose to mark this place on the line?

What are two or three steps you could take toward growing as a disciple?

DISCIPLESHIP

About being disciples
by Nelson Roth

There are two parts of discipleship - "making disciples and being a disciple." Both are vital, and it's important to understand the difference.

"Making disciples" is what Christians are commanded to do in the Great Commission. *"Therefore go and make disciples..."* Matthew 28:19-20. In this passage of scripture we are encouraged to multiply and make other disciples.

On the other hand, being a disciple is about the lifelong process of following Christ and striving to become more like him.

Discipleship is about a Christian's personal relationship with Christ. Ultimately, when a Christian's life is growing, he or she experiences life changing outcomes - in short, transformation.

> *"A disciple is not above his teacher, but everyone when he is fully trained will be like his teacher."* Luke 6:40

The word "disciple" literally means, a learner. According to Vine's Expository Dictionary Of New Testament Words, a disciple is "one who follows another's teaching." A disciple is not only a learner, but also an enthusiast and a devotee.

How would you describe your relationship with Christ?

George Barna in Growing True Disciples says, *"What would happen for God's Kingdom if we [Christian churches, their leaders and members] did not consider our job complete when people confess their sin and say a prayer inviting Jesus to be their Redeemer, but would use their new commitments to Christ as a launching pad for a lifelong quest to become individuals who are completely sold out-emotionally, intellectually, physically, and spiritually-to the Son of God?"* (pg. 2)

In his book, Barna describes research conducted over a two-year period on the state of discipleship and opportunities for effective discipling. His data also included an examination of churches that are doing a great job in growing disciples. **The book's research revealed that less than one out of every five born again adults have any specific and measurable goals related to their personal spiritual development.**

How are you doing as far as "being a disciple"?

How would you articulate the difference of "making disciples" and "being a disciple?"

What personal adjustments would be helpful for you in this matter of "being a disciple"?

I'll wrap up these thoughts on discipleship by sharing shifts that Barna suggests for ministry in the church to be more balanced in these two different areas of discipleship - "making and being."

- Shift from a program-driven ministry to a people-driven ministry
- Change from emphasis on building consensus to building character
- De-emphasize recalling Bible stories, emphasize applying biblical principles
- Move from a concern about quantity (people, programs, square footage, dollars) to a concern about quality (commitment, wisdom, relationships, values, lifestyle)
- Retool developmental ministry efforts from being unrelated and haphazard to being intentional and strategic
- Replace ministry designed to pass on knowledge to efforts intended to facilitate holistic ministry
- Alter people's focus from engaging in the optimal feel-good activities to absolute commitment to personal growth, ministry and authenticity in their faith

Being a disciple is about relationship; relationship with Christ that goes beyond knowing him as personal Savior to an ongoing daily walk of following him and becoming more like him.

Which of the above shifts challenges you the most?

What difference might that shift make in your life and in your ministry?

How and when would you start making such a shift?

DISCIPLESHIP

The journey of discipleship
by Brad Houchin

How would you describe your journey of discipleship?

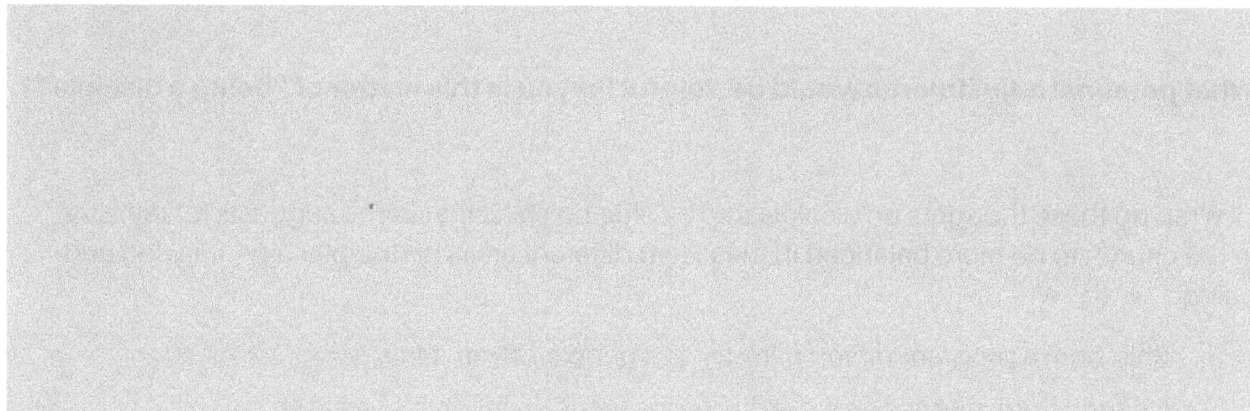

Think for a moment about the incredible journey it must have been to be one of the disciples of Jesus. They walked with him and were eyewitnesses to the miracles he performed. In the Bible, we read about the cost of discipleship and the response that Jesus asks of those who want to follow him.

Imagine Jesus looking directly into your eyes, and being challenged with these words from Luke 14:25-35.

> "Large crowds were traveling with Jesus, and turning to them he said: If anyone comes to me and does not hate father and mother, wife and children, brothers and sisters—yes, even their own life—**such a person cannot be my disciple.** And whoever does not carry their cross and follow me **cannot be my disciple.** Suppose one of you wants to build a tower. Won't you first sit down and estimate the cost to see if you have enough money to complete it? For if you lay the foundation and are not able to finish it, everyone who sees it will ridicule you, saying, This person began to build and wasn't able to finish. Or suppose a king is about to go to war against another king. Won't he first sit down and consider whether he is able with ten thousand men to oppose the one coming against him with twenty thousand? If he is not able, he will send a delegation while the other is still a long way off and will ask for terms of peace. In the same way, **those of you who do not give up everything you have cannot be my disciples.** Salt is good, but if it loses its saltiness, how can it be made salty again? It is fit neither for the soil nor for the manure pile; it is thrown out. Whoever has ears to hear, let them hear."

I wonder how many in the crowd that day heard Jesus' words and just turned and walked away? How many counted the cost and decided it was too high of a price?

How do you think you would have responded to his words if you were a part of the crowd that day?

As Nelson stated in the previous discipleship article, **"Being a disciple, is about the lifelong process of following Christ and striving to become more like him."** Not just reading about how to become more like Christ; but taking action, responding and being more like Christ in all we do and say.

> Matthew 16:24-27, *"Then Jesus said to his disciples, Whoever wants to be my disciple must deny themselves and take up their cross and follow me. For whoever wants to save their life will lose it, but whoever loses their life for me will find it. What good will it be for someone to gain the whole world, yet forfeit their soul? Or what can anyone give in exchange for their soul? For the Son of Man is going to come in his Father's glory with his angels, and then he will reward each person according to what they have done."*

Jesus does not ask for a little bit, or even a lot from us... he asks for ALL!

What is God asking of you on your journey of discipleship and how will you respond?

Just as Jesus looked into the eyes of people and boldly asked them to follow him; he is boldly asking you to do the same.

What will you say, about joining Christ in the journey of discipleship?

DISCIPLESHIP

Revealing the good news of Jesus Christ
by Jeff Hegstrom

Every time I read John 3:16, I am deeply reminded that God's heart is to reveal himself to a world he loves. In the Bible, God's heart and plan for redemption are revealed to us. God's desire is that all mankind would know him and be in relationship with him through his one and only Son, Jesus Christ. That is the good news, the gospel - the hope of glory!

Every year as my family gathers together to celebrate Christmas, I am reminded how God intentionally revealed himself, his love and his desire to be with us, through the birth of his one and only Son, Jesus Christ. The good news was declared through angels to Joseph and Mary, Zechariah and Elizabeth, the shepherds, and he even used a star to lead and reveal the Savior of the world to the wise men.

When Jesus was older and planning to begin his ministry, he went to John the Baptist to be baptized. And when John saw Jesus approaching, John said,"...*the reason I came baptizing with water was that he might be revealed to Israel."* John 1:31

During the time Jesus was physically walking and ministering on the earth, he clearly understood the mission God had given him. Luke 4:43, *"I must proclaim the good news of the kingdom of God to the other towns also, because that is why I was sent."*

Today, God chooses to reveal himself and his glory through you! In the fourteenth chapter of the book of John, Jesus told his disciples that very soon he was going to leave earth to be with his father and not to be troubled or afraid by what was about to take place. In fact, Jesus encouraged them by telling them what they should expect. Take a minute to look up the following verses and then journal your discoveries about how God chooses to reveal himself and his glory through you.

John 14:12-14; John 14:26-27; Matthew 28:18-20; Acts 1:8

As a disciple of Jesus Christ, are you compelled to fully understand the mission he has given us? **Being a disciple of Jesus Christ is about revealing God's glory in everything we say and do.** It is genuinely and authentically living out our everyday life in a way that truly reflects the hope of glory, the good news, so the world may not only see him, but come to know him through the reflection of Jesus Christ in you.

Colossians 1:27, *"To them God has chosen to make known among the Gentiles the glorious riches of this mystery, which is Christ in you, the hope of glory."*

Will you stop right here for a couple minutes to read, pray and reflect on how you could live out the following verses genuinely and authentically in your everyday life? Let God reveal his heart to you and ask him how he wants to reveal his glory in you and in all that you do.

Matthew 5:16 , *"In the same way, let your light shine before men, that they may see your good deeds and praise your Father in heaven."*

John 15:8, *"This is to my Father's glory, that you bear much fruit, showing yourselves to be my disciples."*

1 Corinthians 10:31-33. *"So whether you eat or drink or whatever you do, do it all for the glory of God. Do not cause anyone to stumble, whether Jews, Greeks or the church of God— even as I try to please everyone in every way. For I am not seeking my own good but the good of many, so that they may be saved."*

What was one practical thing God revealed as you read these verses?

Taking it deeper:

- Take a minute to recall how God revealed the good news to you?

- Who were the people in your life that he used to reveal his great love and his desire to have a relationship with you through his one and only Son, Jesus Christ?

- Was it spoken words and/or actions that revealed God's glory and his love?

- As a disciple of Jesus Christ...How are you living in a way that is revealing the hope of glory in you?

Final thought: As a father of three boys, I am often reminded and challenged not only by the power of the words I choose to speak, but by the power of my actions. What I have discovered is "actions speak louder than words!"

Living in community with others
by Brad Houchin

From the beginning, living in community has been God's designed plan for mankind. We were not only created to be in relationship with God, but also with other people.

Right now, take a few moments to consider relationships within your community.

Who is a part of your community?

Where do you find your community?

What impact do you have on or in your community?

What is the impact that your community has on you?

Our culture promotes relationships to provide a comfort level for us, saying we should only take a risk when we feel like it or when we need something from someone. What did Jesus teach and model for his followers?

> Matthew 9:35-38, *"Jesus went through all the towns and villages, teaching in their synagogues, proclaiming the good news of the kingdom and healing every disease and sickness. When he saw the crowds, he had compassion on them, because they were harassed and helpless, like sheep without a shepherd. Then Jesus said to his disciples, "'The harvest is plentiful but the workers are few. Ask the Lord of the harvest, therefore, to send out workers into his harvest field.'"*

While Jesus was ministering on earth, he modeled how to have a right balance in community. Like Jesus, it is important for us to not just be focused on our "church community." We need to look for opportunities to spread the truth of God's Word by being in relationship with others outside of our "church community." As we surround ourselves with those who are like-minded in faith, we engage in "iron sharpening iron" kinds of relationships. At the same time, we also need to be intentional to engage in relationship with those in need; praying that Christ will be revealed.

How does your community compare to the example set by Jesus?

What is the importance of being involved in a community of like-minded believers?

Who is in your "iron sharpening iron" community and what is the impact he/she has on you?

Jesus was intentional in reaching out to others. We too, need this same intentionality in building our communities. Often, we can struggle not knowing how to connect with certain people, especially those who might not share all of the same values and beliefs that we have. Others might be hard to connect with because we cannot directly relate to what they may be going through or we may not have a way to directly meet their needs. In the end though, we have exactly what they need, and we need to trust God has placed them in our lives for this very purpose.

> Acts 3:3-10, *"One day Peter and John were going up to the temple at the time of prayer—at three in the afternoon. Now a man who was lame from birth was being carried to the temple gate called Beautiful, where he was put every day to beg from those going into the temple courts. When he saw Peter and John about to enter, he asked them for money. Peter looked straight at him, as did John. Then Peter said, 'Look at us!' So the man gave them his attention, expecting to get something from them. Then Peter said, 'Silver or gold I do not have, but what I do have I give you. In the name of Jesus Christ of Nazareth, walk.' Taking him by the right hand, he helped him up, and instantly the man's feet and ankles became strong. He jumped to his feet and began to walk. Then he went with them into the temple courts, walking and jumping, and praising God. When all the people saw him walking and praising God, they recognized him as the same man who used to sit begging at the temple gate called Beautiful, and they were filled with wonder and amazement at what had happened to him."*

We have the hope of Christ to share! It is in sharing this message that we have `confidence to influence and impact our community - those who are *like-minded* in faith, and those who are hurting and lost.

What makes living in community relevant for you?

commUNITY, and its outcome
by Nelson Roth

In my ministry role, I have the privilege of connecting with pastors and other church leaders. What's awesome about connecting with these leaders around the Relevant Discipleship Pathway is our common denominator. It isn't a particular denomination; but, rather a love of Jesus Christ and his Word.

Recently, I was sitting with a pastor in his office for a discipleship session and in the middle of our time together, out of the blue, he said, "This is really good ... connecting and having the conversations that we are having; I really need this." He went on to say, "Before you reached out to me, we were in our own 'silos', doing our own thing; and to think, we lived just fifteen minutes apart and now we are united and experiencing community."

There was such unity in the room that day. My pastor friend and I were experiencing real biblical commUNITY! Today, we are both growing spiritually and we are being encouraged in our ministry and personal lives because of our continued friendship.

Jesus is our example of serving and living in unity among others. On the night before going to the cross, Jesus prayed. In his prayer, found in John 17, he expressed his heart. His disciples and those who would become followers in the years to come were his primary concern. His desire was they would live in unity!

He said to God the Father in verse 11, "*protect them by the power of your name - the name you gave me - so that they may be one as we are one.*" The heart of the Father and Jesus Christ the Son, is that we as believers, would live together in unity.

The early church raised the bar concerning commUNITY, giving us an example. In Acts 2:42, "*They devoted themselves to the apostles' teaching and to the fellowship, to the breaking of bread and to prayer.*" The early church spent a lot of time together in commUNITY. Verse 44 says, when they got together there were no distinctions or discriminations - "*all that believed were together and had all things common.*"

How do you do commUNITY?

If the early church is an example for commUNITY for us, what would you like to experience?

The word fellowship that's found in Acts 2:42, means *sharing*. The believers of the early church lived life together in close relationships and freely shared with one another.

How is it possible for you to experience commUNITY?

God through others is equipping his people, *"for works of service, so that the body of Christ may be built up until we all reach unity in the faith and in the knowledge of the Son of God and become mature, attaining to the whole measure of the fullness of Christ."* Ephesians 4:12-13

As we *"become mature, attaining to the whole measure of the fullness of Christ;"* we grow in Christ and we grow in unity.

So then, what hinders commUNITY?

If it's about growth, commUNITY would be limited by the the degree of willingness to grow spiritually by the various individuals of a group.

Why is it so important to fully understand commUNITY and make it a part of our experience?

Paul wrote a letter to the divided believers in Corinth. Believers were allowing a disagreement to hinder their fellowship. Paul says in 1 Corinthians chapter one, verse 10, we are obligated to *"agree with one another in what you (we) say and that there be no divisions among you (us), but that you (we) be perfectly united in mind and thought."* Why was this so important? Paul says in verse seventeen, *"lest the cross of Christ be emptied of its power."*

How could our relationship with other believers impact positively or negatively our mission?

In contrast to Corinth, here is what is recorded about the believers of the early church in Acts chapter two, verse 42, they were *"praising God and enjoying the favor of all the people. And the Lord added to their number daily those who were being saved."*

How is God speaking to you about relating to believers in your commUNITY?

What would you like to see different in your life over the next few months?

What steps can you take to move in that direction?

A healthy community is compelled to respond
by Jeff Hegstrom

I love that the gospel of Jesus Christ is such a uniting factor. The truth is we are all sinners saved by grace through faith in Jesus Christ.

That is the beauty of the cross. It doesn't matter who you are or where you have been, your nationality, your job or your financial status. Galatians 3:28, *"There is neither Jew nor Greek, slave nor free, male nor female, for you are all one in Christ Jesus."*

We are all one in Christ for those who believed and place our trust in Jesus Christ for salvation. Paul writes in Ephesians 4:4-6, *"There is one body and one Spirit–just as you were called to one hope when you were called – one Lord, one faith, one baptism; one God and Father of all, who is over all and through all and in all."*

When I think of COMMUNITY, my first response is to think of the early church from Acts 2 and how they gathered daily to study God's Word, pray and do life together. But one thing really stands out for me about this group of believers ... they genuinely cared about each other and were concerned about the needs they saw around them. In Acts 2:44-45, *"All the believers were together and had everything in common. Selling their possessions and goods, they gave to anyone as he had need."* This community of believers saw the needs that existed around them and were compelled to RESPOND by selling their possessions and goods; and giving freely to anyone who had a need.

What compelled this community of believers to be so willing to RESPOND to those in need?

When it comes down to it, it can be summed up in these three powerful and life transforming words ..."God's extravagant love!"

This kind of love compels you and I to RESPOND with compassion and generosity; which comes from the overflow of our relationship with God. As we "KNOW" God, we begin to truly understand the extravagance and generosity of his great love. He saved us and set us free from our sin and has given us eternal life through Christ's death, burial and resurrection. Knowing this, we cannot help but to RESPOND and allow his love to flow out of our lives, our attitudes, and our actions into all of our relationships with others!

> 1 John 4:10-11, *"This is love: not that we loved God, but that he loved us and sent his Son as an atoning sacrifice for our sins. Dear friends, since God so loved us, we also ought to love one another."*
>
> 1 John 4:19, *"We love because he first loved us."*
>
> 2 Corinthians 5:14, *"For Christ's love compels us, because we are convinced that one died for all..."*

How does God's love compel you to RESPOND?

How are you RESPONDING to those who have a need in your COMMUNITY?

> 2 Corinthians 8:2-6, *"Out of the most severe trial, their overflowing joy and their extreme poverty welled up in rich generosity. For I testify that they gave as much as they were able, and even beyond their ability. Entirely on their own, they urgently pleaded with us for the privilege of sharing in this service to the saints. And they did not do as we expected, but they gave themselves first to the Lord and then to us in keeping with God's will."*
>
> Verse 7, *"But just as you excel in everything-in faith, in speech, in knowledge, in complete earnestness and in your love for us-see that you also excel in this grace of giving."*

COMMUNITY

Where two or more are gathered
by Nelson Roth

Christian community happens when followers of Christ get together. On weekends, believers gather for a corporate experience of worship and the word. Throughout the week as life goes on, believers share life in various ways with one another.

These times together can be awesome, and what makes them uniquely special is the presence of the Lord! Whether the gathering is large or small, when Christ, by his Spirit shows up, there is an awareness that you're connected with God during that time of community.

> *"For where two or three come together in my name, there am I with them."* Matthew 18:20

Christ has promised to be *"with us always."* And yes, the presence of God happens when we're alone with him; but, we also need the community experience and the impact it has on our lives.

The Word teaches us, we *"are being built together to become a dwelling in which God lives by his Spirit."* Ephesians 2:19-22

How have you seen Christ revealed with other believers in your community?

As a pastor, I remember being overly concerned at times about first time visitors coming to our church. My concern was whether they would be comfortable with or understand our style of worship. Interestingly, a visitor actually helped me with this. He said after attending a worship service, he wasn't familiar with all that took place; however, he sensed the presence of God. Then he took the next incredible step by saying, "Today, my experience made me realize that I really don't know God and I want to receive Christ as my Savior!"

Through this experience, I got beyond being overly concerned and learned to trust Christ and the power of the Holy Spirit. He is the one in our midst and he impacts us when we, as believers, are gathered together in community.

"But I, when I am lifted up from the earth, will draw all men to myself." John 12:32

When did you become a believer and begin your walk with Christ?

As a believer, how do you experience Christian community?

When you gather with two or more, how have you been transformed by Christ being revealed to you?

COMMUNITY

Commissioned to go
by Brad Houchin

What is the first thought that comes to your mind when you hear the word evangelism?

Do you get excited and pumped up about the opportunity to share Christ with others? Maybe you get somewhat nervous or even a little frightful at the thought of having to share your faith with someone?

Why does it seem that evangelism comes so easy for some like they were made for it; and for others, it can be as nerve racking or frightening as going to the dentist, or standing on the edge of a steep cliff looking down?

If you're like me, you instantly think of evangelism as standing on the street corner or going door to door in a neighborhood telling people about Jesus. That thought, quite honestly, can cause me to freak out! Yet, I have come to learn over time, that I have completely missed the mark on what evangelism is. God has not only called me; but, he has also equipped me for evangelism. Gratefully it does not mean I have to stand on a street corner or knock on doors.

In the Great Commission, Matthew 28:19, we are commanded to *"go and make disciples."*

We are told to go throughout all the nations to evangelize. But **there is so much more to this than it being a command.** We have also been **commissioned** by Jesus to fulfill this command.

What is the difference between being commanded and being commissioned for a command?

You see, Jesus does not just tell us to "go." He has commissioned us to "go." We have been given the authority and granted permission by Jesus Christ to carry out the work he started. Jesus has equipped us with everything we need for evangelism. We have been given all the power and authority we need for carrying out the Great Commission and evangelism.

Read the following passages of scripture and answer the questions.

- **What is the promise in this passage of scripture?**

- **How does this passage of scripture empower you and encourage you in your part of carrying out the Great Commission?**

John 14:12-14, *"Very truly I tell you, whoever believes in me will do the works I have been doing, and they will do even greater things than these, because I am going to the Father. And I will do whatever you ask in my name, so that the Father may be glorified in the Son. You may ask me for anything in my name, and I will do it."*

Acts 3:6-8, *"Then Peter said, 'Silver or gold I do not have, but what I do have I give you. In the name of Jesus Christ of Nazareth, walk.' Taking him by the right hand, he helped him up, and instantly the man's feet and ankles became strong. He jumped to his feet and began to walk."*

Romans 12:3-8, *"For by the grace given me I say to every one of you: Do not think of yourself more highly than you ought, but rather think of yourself with sober judgment, in accordance with the faith God has distributed to each of you. For just as each of us has one body with many members, and these members do not all have the same function, so in Christ we, though many, form one body, and each member belongs to all the others. We have different gifts, according to the grace given to each of us. If your gift is prophesying, then prophesy in accordance with your faith; if it is serving, then serve; if it is teaching, then teach; if it is to encourage, then give encouragement; if it is giving, then give generously; if it is to lead, do it diligently; if it is to show mercy, do it cheerfully."*

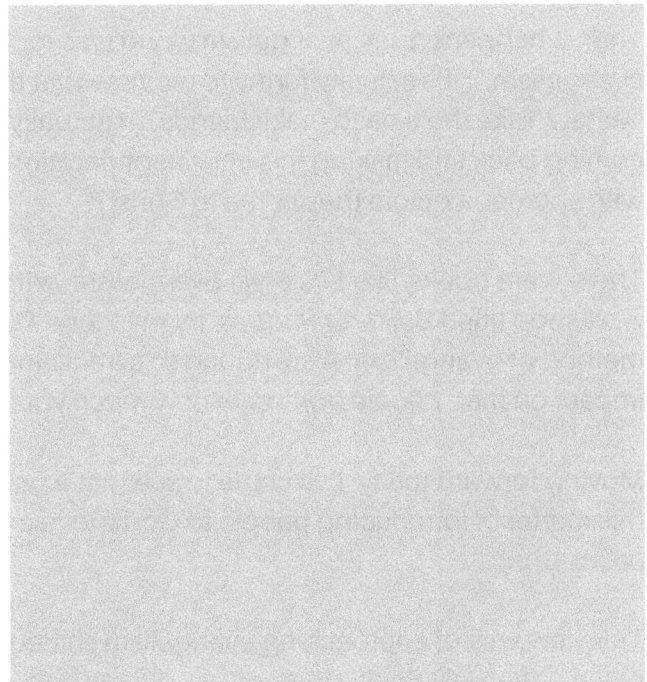

You have been commissioned to 'go and make disciples'. For each one of us our 'go place' might look a little different than others. The important thing is that we have a 'go place' and that God has empowered us and equipped us for that place. At home, work, school, throughout the neighborhood, even across the ocean ... *"the harvest is plentiful."*

Are you ready to go and make disciples?

EVANGELISM

Friendship evangelism
by Nelson Roth

In the early years of my ministry, my evangelism experiences placed an emphasis on the "go" of "making disciples." Evangelism was about soul winning, which meant handing out tracts, talking to strangers, and presenting what was called the Romans Road to Salvation. The process usually started out with a question ... "If you were to die today, where would you spend eternity?"

God in many cases blessed and used this method with new converts being baptized and continuing to follow Christ. Also, there were those who prayed a prayer and that was it.

I'm sure it was also possible there were others who felt offended because of the approach, turned off, and as a result missed the love and grace God wanted them to experience.

Then it happened, my evangelism world was rocked. I started to hear about "friendship evangelism." It's actually funny to me now that this approach seemed so radical back then. "What? Take the time to make friends?" I actually resisted with the justification that, "Jesus is coming back and making this important decision is urgent! Who has time to build a relationship with someone before they come to Christ?"

There were books, like *Life-Style Evangelism* written by Joseph Aldridge back in 1981 and workshop titled *Building Bridges*, by my friend Dan Woodard; which broke ground for this new method of evangelism. Also, during this transition process, I picked up this slogan that had an impact on me, *"people don't care how much you know until they know how much you care."*

Moving forward today, I've come to see that a genuine relationship with others is essential in this matter of introducing people to God's love and his redemption provided through his Son, Jesus Christ.

This new way of approaching evangelism shifted responsibility for the outcome to its rightful place ... the Holy Spirit. I learned as I did my part, that I had One in partnership with me who would do his. Now, Jesus' words in John 6:44 make sense, *"No one can come to me unless the Father who sent me draws him."*

How does friendship or relational evangelism sound to you?

It's really about living life on mission 24/7. Genuinely making friends and growing authentic relationships with others by letting the light of Christ shine in our daily routines. Then, taking opportunity to share when it's invited; and, being direct at the right times when we've earned the right to do so.

"How can they hear without someone preaching to them?" Romans 10:14.

Who are you building a genuine relationship with right now?

"But in your hearts set apart Christ as Lord. Always be prepared to give an answer to everyone who asks you to give the reason for the hope that you have. But do this with gentleness and respect." 1 Peter 3:15

EVANGELISM

An open door
by Brad Houchin

Several years ago, I was able to spend two days in a nearby city serving families who had been greatly affected by a tornado. The path of destruction left behind by the storm changed the lives of many families; and it took months, and even years, for parts of that city to be completely rebuilt.

A tornado or any natural disaster creates a large physical need for response. At one point, I had stopped working and looked down the road at all the volunteers. Many were carrying food and water to families and other volunteers; while others were working in the home and yards of the people they were serving.

I remember as though it were today, the sounds of chainsaws cutting trees off of cars and homes, blue tarps being nailed to roofs to cover holes, raking and clearing debris from yards, and crews completely emptying some homes of all of the contents and hauling them to the side of the road for trash. I also noticed church vans from all over Mississippi, Alabama, Louisiana, Arkansas, Florida and Missouri. I was simply in awe that day of God's church as it was responding relevantly to the needs of this community.

A relevant response to a need opens the door for evangelism.

Everyone has needs and we all need others to respond to our needs at times. Some may need food or a drink, or even a place to lay their head at night; while others may need help with an overwhelming project or simply a friend who will listen and be there for them. One need connects us all together, and that is our need for a relationship with Jesus Christ.

What are the needs of those around you ... family, friends, coworkers, and neighbors?

Like the example of the woman at the well Jesus gives us in John 4, a relevant response to a need opens the door for evangelism.

John 4:10-15, "If you knew the gift of God and who it is that asks you for a drink, you would have asked him and he would have given you living water." "Sir," the woman said, "you have nothing to draw with and the well is deep. Where can you get this living water? Are you greater than our father Jacob, who gave us the well and drank from it himself, as did also his sons and his livestock?" Jesus answered, "Everyone who drinks this water will be thirsty again, but whoever drinks the water I give them will never thirst. Indeed, the water I give them will become in them a spring of water welling up to eternal life." The woman said to him, "Sir, give me this water so that I won't get thirsty and have to keep coming here to draw water."

The door for evangelism was been flung wide open in the city where I volunteered. There is a huge opportunity in these types of natural disaster situations to reach a city for Christ; and, it goes way beyond putting a blue tarp on a roof and cutting up a tree. But often, it takes meeting a person right at their point of need ... then, we can speak to their spiritual need of entering into a relationship with Jesus Christ.

What are some ways you can respond to the needs of people around you?

How might your right response to these needs open the door for you to share their need for Christ?

How will you respond?

Your conversion story reveals the glory of God
by Jeff Hegstrom

One of the things I really enjoy about serving with Relevant Ministry is working with our interns. As part of our leadership training, we spend 40 weeks with our long term interns going through a leadership curriculum, *Charting a Bold Course* by Andrew Seidel, to equip them to be the leaders God has called them to be. This is also an opportunity to prepare them for life and future ministry opportunities that God may lead them to.

Although I enjoy teaching all of the sessions, I particularly enjoy leading our session on "The Leader's Life Story." Together, we spend a week writing and mapping out the key events in our lives and discovering the life lessons in them. Then we look at how God has used every event and circumstance to shape and mold us into the person we are today. Whether our life events were joyful or painful, good or bad, God never wastes anything in our lives when we surrender to him.

The following week, we as leaders and interns share our life stories. It's a powerful time in which we laugh, weep and celebrate together what God has done in our lives. For me, this is one of the most significant sessions in our training. For many, they see for the first time how God has been there all along, through every circumstance ... drawing us to him.

God's love is so vast, so deep, that he never stops loving us and pursuing us with his everlasting love. When you finally recognize God's hand in your life, it changes everything; and, you can't wait to reveal Christ to others by sharing your conversion story.

There are two things I have discovered while teaching this session; firstly, **people like stories.** Who doesn't like to sit down and listen to a good story? Jesus understood and modeled this in his ministry. As people gathered around Jesus, he often used stories or parables to teach about what the kingdom of God was like. Stories help us relate to one another and what is going on in our lives around us.

Secondly, I have discovered that **every believer has a powerful conversion story;** which is part of their life story. How many times have we been talking to someone and they share a personal example from their own life about what you were just talking about?

Just like the interns discovered, God has given every believer their own personal life story. It's a story of his amazing, redeeming love and how he has been there all along through every circumstance and event you have experienced in your life to draw you to him.

How do you see God's response to you as you begin to consider your conversion story?

How will you respond?

Now, God wants you to share your conversion story with others he has placed in your life. Whether it's through the relationships you have built or in those times that you respond to others in need. **Your unique conversion story is a story God wants to use through you to reveal himself and offer hope to the world!**

> Romans 10:13-15, *"Everyone who calls on the name of the Lord will be saved."* How, then, can they call on the one they have not believed in? And how can they believe in the one of whom they have not heard? And how can they hear without someone preaching to them? And how can they preach unless they are sent? As it is written, *"How beautiful are the feet of those who bring good news!"*

What's your conversion story? Will you take some time to sit down and write out your story? What have been key events in your life? What did you learn from those specific experiences? How has God used those experiences in your life to form and shape you into the person you are today?

Go share the story God has given you and let God's glory be revealed through you!

EVANGELISM

coaching
tools

Instructions:

Coaching is an integral part of Relevant Discipleship™. By applying three key coaching techniques ... good listening skills, asking powerful questions, and following through with action and accountability, you can experience discipleship coaching with someone else and you can use the skill of self coaching during your personal time of reflection. If you would like to learn more about coaching, you may want to read the book, *Nehemiah Response ... a coaching model* by Nelson and Pam Roth.

In this section, you will have an opportunity to take each of the 7 disciplines deeper by considering the powerful questions of each coaching tool. As you focus on one particular discipline for several weeks, use the coaching tool for the discipline along with the corresponding four articles during your personal time of reflection. Remember, the more you participate in the process, the greater the spiritual benefits.

Coaching Tools for the 7 disciplines: titles and descriptions

WORSHIP is more than music
God is truly worthy of our worship! Discover what worship is, ways to worship the Lord, and how worship can be a lifestyle.

How to pray, a pattern for PRAYER
With this coaching tool, you will be able to experience the pattern of prayer Jesus taught his disciples; and be challenged with questions that could bring your prayer life to another level.

8 steps to reading the WORD
Along with offering suggestions for getting started each time you read the Bible, this coaching tool helps to put a focus on "quality over quantity" when you read the Word.

Use the gift you received to serve through MINISTRY

The description for the discipline of Ministry is discovering spiritual gifts and serving like Christ. This coaching tool will help you become aware of how your spiritual gifts can empower your ministry.

Live with integrity as a DISCIPLE of Christ

The Discipleship discipline is about 'being' more than 'doing'. Character and 'who' we are is the starting place for the discipline of Discipleship and 'who' we are gives credibility to 'what we do'.

Implementing the 'one anothers' into your COMMUNITY

As you practice the discipline of Community with other believers, be thinking about the 'fellowship of believers' and be looking for opportunities to experience fellowship and Community with others like the believers in Acts 2 who 'devoted themselves ... to fellowship'.

EVANGELISM and making disciples

When you hear the word 'evangelism' what comes to mind? Who/what do you think of? A question that's raised in this coaching tool is, "When sharing Christ with someone, what is your starting point to connect with them?"

Psalm 100:2, *"Serve the Lord with gladness! Come into his presence with singing."*

Along with singing, what other action is seen in the verse above?

What is it God desires and what are the ways you worship him?

I remember an illustration, given by Peter Lord during a pastor's retreat my wife and I attended. Peter was a deep thinking, contemplative type person who knew God intimately. His teachings were often illustrated with simple dry humor; which helped in remembering the point behind the story. In one such story, when he was teaching about true worship, he asked the question, "How do you know what God wants?" Peter said, "If you know God likes pie and you assume it is cherry pie, and you bring him cherry pie all of your life. How would you feel when you get to heaven, and you learn his favorite pie is pumpkin?"

What is the point of the pie story?

Besides music and singing, how do you worship God?

Romans 12:1,*"present your bodies as a living sacrifice, holy and **acceptable** unto God, which is your spiritual worship."*

Our worship is giving to God what's acceptable. Acceptable, yoo-ar'-es-tos, in Greek, means that which is pleasing – it's a term of worship.

How acceptable is your spiritual act of worship?

This Greek word, yoo-ar'-es-tos, found ten times in the New Testament, boils down to four specific actions about what God wants. **How does each of these 'acceptable to God' actions speak to you?**

1 Romans 14:18, *"Anyone who serves Christ is acceptable to God and approved by men."* All of Romans chapter 14 is about helping a weaker brother to not stumble.

How is your service and love for others a form of worship?

2 Romans 15:16 talks about Paul being a minister of Christ to the Gentiles and taking the message of the gospel to them, *"...in the priestly service of the gospel of God, so that the offering of the Gentiles may be acceptable."*

How is leading someone to Christ an act of worship?

3 Philippians 4:18, Paul writes about an offering of financial provision brought to him, *"...the gifts you sent, a fragrant offering, a sacrifice acceptable and pleasing to God."*

How generous are you with your resources ... time, natural gifts, spiritual gifts, finances?

4 Ephesians 5:10, *"...to discern what is pleasing (acceptable) to the Lord."* What's the issue here? Verse 8 reads, *"...for at one time you were darkness, but now you are light in the Lord. Walk as children of light."* This is speaking of godliness and holiness.

Since holiness is an act of worship, where are you on your personal journey of godliness and holiness?

In what ways are you challenged in these four acts of worship?

What shifts will you make so your worship is more than a weekend event?

Suggested Reading:
The Air I Breathe: worship as a way of life, Louie Giglio
Worship: The Missing Jewel, A. W. Tozer

Watch a training video for disciple makers about this coaching tool.
www.relevantministry.org/relevantdiscipleship

Jesus said in Matthew 6:9-13, *"This, then, is how you should pray."*

This prayer, commonly referred to as The Lord's Prayer can be memorized and recited; however, what happens if we see it as a pattern for our prayers? Out of the verses from Matthew 6:9-13, Jesus teaches the disciples 'how to pray'. How might the five themes identified below enhance your communication with God?

To practice the discipline of Prayer around the five themes; in the boxes below, write out some thoughts you can pray. When you pray Jesus' pattern for prayer, how can you verbalize your thoughts in prayer around each of the five themes?

v.9 *Our Father in heaven, hallowed be your name*

❶

How might you express adoration and praise?
Paul and Silas prayed and praised God even when put in prison – Acts 16:25

v.10 *Your kingdom come, your will be done, on earth as it is in heaven*

❷

What is God's plan for you today?
(Jesus) "...not my will, but Thy will be done" – Matthew 26:39

v.11 *Give us today our daily bread*

❸

What is your request today?
We are encouraged to let our requests be known to God - Philippians 4:6

v.12 *And forgive us our debts, as we also have forgiven our debtors*

④

What do you need to ask forgiveness for today?
Believers are cleansed of daily sins and find pardon by the blood of Jesus - 1 John 1:7-10

v.13 *And lead us not into temptation, but deliver us from the evil one*

⑤

What steps are you taking to put on the armor?
When we put on Christ, we put on and find protection from the Armor of God
– Romans 13:14; Ephesians 6:10-18

> *Prayer is a sincere, sensible, affectionate pouring out of the heart or soul to God, through Christ, in the strength and assistance of the Holy Spirit, for such things as God has promised, or according to his Word, for the good of the church, with submission in faith to the will of God.*
> *Prayer*, John Bunyan

How can these five themes help you when you pray?

What one new habit would you like to make part of your regular prayer discipline?

Suggested Reading:
Lord, Teach Us to Pray, Andrew Murray
The Necessity of Prayer, E. M. Bounds

Watch a training video for disciple makers about this coaching tool.
www.relevantministry.org/relevantdiscipleship

1. Before you read, confess known sin - 1 John 1:9

2. Pray for any unknown sin to be revealed - Psalm 139:23-24

3. Remove preconceived ideas - Isaiah 55:8

4. Read, knowing the Holy Spirit is your teacher - John 14:26

5. Read until God stops you - John 16:13

6. Write verse(s) down that stand out to you - Jeremiah 31:33

7. Meditate on the verse(s) - Joshua 1:8

8. Ask this question, "Lord, what do you want me to do?" - John 14:15

How could the Bible come alive and be relevant for your life with these eight steps?

Each verse below aligns with the 8 steps above.

1. *"But if we confess our sins to him, he is faithful and just to forgive us and to cleanse us from every wrong."* 1 John 1:9 NLT

2. *"Search me, O God, and know my heart; test me and know my thoughts. Point out anything in me that offends you, and lead me along the path of everlasting life."* Psalm 139:23-24 NLT

3. *"My thoughts are completely different from yours," says the Lord. "And my ways are far beyond anything you could imagine."* Isaiah 55:8 NLT

4. *"But when the Father sends the Counselor as my representative – and by the Counselor I mean the Holy Spirit – he will teach you everything and will remind you of everything I myself have told you."* John 14:26 NLT

5. *"When the Spirit of truth comes, he will guide you into all truth. He will not be presenting his own ideas; he will be telling you what he has heard. He will tell you about the future."* John 16:13 NLT

6. *"But this is the new covenant I will make with the people of Israel on that day," says the Lord. "I will put my laws in their minds, and I will write them on their hearts. I will be their God, and they will be my people."* Jeremiah 31:33 NLT

7. *"Study this Book of the Law continually. Meditate on it day and night so you may be sure to obey all that is written in it. Only then will you succeed."* Joshua 1:8 NLT

8. *"If you love me, obey my commandments."* John 14:15 NLT

What is God saying to you in the Word today?

What will you do to obey God?

Suggested Reading:
Knowing God, J. I. Packer
Crazy Love: Overwhelmed by a Relentless God, Francis Chan

Watch a training video for disciple makers about this coaching tool.
www.relevantministry.org/relevantdiscipleship

What does this verse have to say about spiritual gifts?

I Peter 4:10-11, *"Each of you should use whatever gift you have received to serve others, as faithful stewards of God's grace in its various forms. If anyone speaks, they should do so as one who speaks the very words of God. If anyone serves, they should do so with the strength God provides, so that in all things God may be praised through Jesus Christ. To him be the glory and the power for ever and ever. Amen."*

Find and underline the seven spiritual gifts found in this passage.

Romans 12:6-8, *"We have different gifts, according to the grace given to each of us. If your gift is prophesying, then prophesy in accordance with your faith; if it is serving, then serve; if it is teaching, then teach; if it is to encourage, then give encouragement; if it is giving, then give generously; if it is to lead, do it diligently; if it is to show mercy, do it cheerfully."*

Here is a very brief description of each spiritual gift found in the passage above:

Prophecy: He or she points out a previous warning or shows what might be wrong. A Christian with this gift may communicate timely and urgent messages which seem to come directly from the Lord and has been told so by people.

Serving: He or she sees a task and gets it done. A Christian with this gift feels more comfortable assisting another person than being up front teaching or leading a group.

Teaching: He or she digs to get the facts to discover answers. A Christian with this gift has been told that they help people learn biblical truth in a meaningful way.

Encouragement: He or she helps others look to the future and the way things can be. A Christian with this gift is particularly apt at helping others process personal problems.

Giving: He or she contributes from their material resources to meet needs. A Christian with this gift gets special delight from providing something for others who could use it. They love to give gifts.

Leadership: He or she promotes working together to achieve goals of the group with the future purpose in mind. A Christian with this gift sees a situation that is disorganized and in need of order or rearrangement and gets excited about being involved in that process.

Showing Mercy: He or she empathizes with the pain of others and extends compassion and Christ's love. A Christian with this gift is moved by people in distress and tries to do something, even if it is listening to relieve the pressure.

After reading the descriptions above, which gift(s) resonates with how you serve?

How do others affirm you when they see you serving?

Suggested Relevant Ministry Workshop:
The 7 gifts of this coaching tool can be referred to as the 'motivational gifts'. There are 25 gifts taught in the **RightFit Ministry Workshop.** Ask your Relevant Discipleship Coach about hosting this workshop at your church. Discoveries are made by participants about how God has uniquely created and given them spiritual gifts, personality and passion to serve him.

Watch a training video for disciple makers about this coaching tool.
www.relevantministry.org/relevantdiscipleship

What do you think of when you hear the word integrity?

In Matthew 5:33-37, Jesus teaches his disciples to live with integrity. His instructions expose the insincerity of people who give weight to their empty promises by using God's name. As a Christ follower we are to both mean and follow through with promises instead of looking for loopholes. We are to be so believable when we speak that we don't need to add something like … "honest to God," to our statement. It's interesting too, that Jesus gives permission to say 'no' as well as instructing us to keep the promises we say 'yes' to.

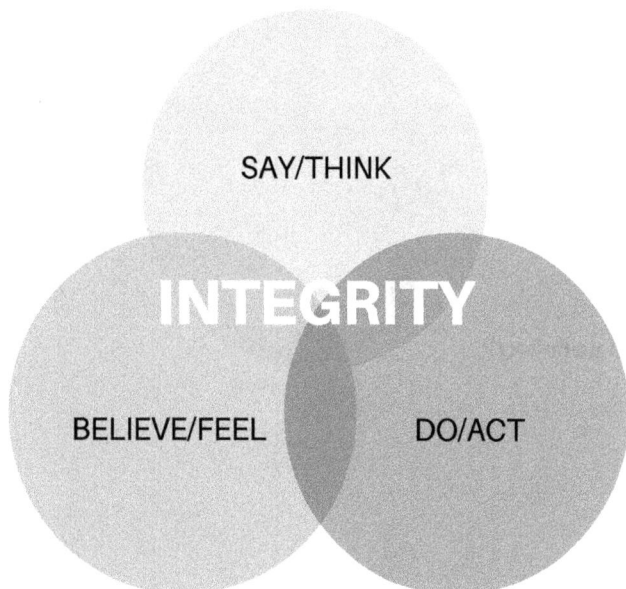

How do the parts of the three circles to the left merge into one circle for you?

SAY/THINK

INTEGRITY

BELIEVE/FEEL   DO/ACT

See the diagram to the left. Integrity has to do with a sense of consistency between a person's inner values/beliefs, their outward words and actions. When there is dissonance between what we say we believe and what we do, there is tension; and that tension creates stress and sometimes a sense of guilt in our lives.

Definition of integrity: the quality of being honest and having strong moral principles; moral uprightness...

honesty, honor, good character, principle(s), ethics, morals, righteousness, morality, virtue, decency, fairness, scrupulousness, sincerity, truthfulness, trustworthiness

The root of the word integrity is integer. Integrity is the state of being whole and undivided.

Definition of integer (the root of integrity): a whole number; a thing complete in itself.

"The integrity of the upright guides them, but the
unfaithful are destroyed by their duplicity."
Proverbs 11:3

How are you challenged in areas of your life with duplicity, or double mindedness?

Unfortunately, in today's society, too many people are living by situational values ... in other words, they are not holding true to their personal values; rather they are allowing the situation to govern how they behave instead of conscientiously choosing to stand firm on what they believe.

What character traits is God's Spirit prompting you as a disciple to grow in?

What really matters to you ... what are your personal values?

How hard is it for you affirmatively to say either 'yes' or 'no' to something?

How might living with integrity give you a sense of purpose?

Adapted from *Charting A Bold Course* by Andrew Seidel

Suggested Relevant Ministry Workshop:
Ask your Relevant Discipleship Coach about hosting the **Discover Your Calling Workshop** at your church. Participants of this workshop move forward from foundational discoveries around personal values, time management, and God's will.

Watch a training video for disciple makers about this coaching tool.
www.relevantministry.org/relevantdiscipleship

DISCIPLESHIP

"From him the whole body, joined and held together by every supporting ligament, grows and builds itself up in love, as each part does its work." Ephesians 4:16

How is the Body of Christ built up?

"My prayer is not for them alone. I pray also for those who will believe in me through their message, that all of them may be one, Father, just as you are in me and I am in you. May they also be in us so that the world may believe that you have sent me."
John 17:20-21

How will you respond to Jesus' prayer in the Garden of Gethsemane for all believers?

Loving one another ·················· Romans 13:8; 1 Thessalonians 3:12; 4:9

Members of one another ··············· Romans 12:5

Devoted to one another ··············· Romans 12:10

Honor one another ··················· Romans 12:10

Be of the same mind with one another ··· Romans 12:16; 15:5

Accept one another ·················· Romans 15:7

Admonish/Instruct one another ········ Romans 15:14

Serve one another ··················· Galatians 5:13

Carrying one another's burdens ······· Galatians 6:2

Bear with one another ················ Ephesians 4:2; Colossians 3:13

Submit to one another ················ Ephesians 5:21; 1 Peter 5:5

Encouraging one another ················· 1 Thessalonians 4:18; 5:11, 14

Edifying one another ···················· Romans 14:19

Greeting one another ··················· Romans 16:16; I Corinthians 16:20

Waiting for one another ················· 1 Corinthians 11:33

Caring for one another ················· 1 Corinthians 12:25

Being kind to one another ············· Ephesians 4:32

Esteeming one another ················· Philippians 2:3

Confessing sins to one another ········ James 5:16

Praying for one another ················· James 5:16

Fellowship with one another ··········· 1 John 1:7

Offering hospitality to one another ····· 1 Peter 4:9

Which one of the 'one anothers' challenges you the most right now?

What action steps can you take to be more like Christ in that area?

COMMUNITY

Suggested Reading:
Building Up One Another, Gene A. Getz

Watch a training video for disciple makers about this coaching tool.
www.relevantministry.org/relevantdiscipleship

Matthew 28:19-20 - the Great Commission

We 'make disciples' by going, baptizing, and teaching. In this coaching tool, Evangelism and making disciples, our focus is on the 'go' and considering evangelism as a process. The 'baptizing' and 'teaching' is on the equipping side of 'making disciples'.

'going'	*'making disciples'*	*'baptizing & teaching'*
EVANGELISM		EQUIPPING

How can we best engage with and reach out to not-yet-believers?

Since evangelism is part of the discipleship process, how can we disciple people to Jesus and on to maturity?

Who do you know that's on the journey to the cross and where are they?

1 (no interest)	2 (curious)	3 (looking)	4 (conversion)

What are your thoughts about the possible places people can be for how they feel about God and Jesus?

When sharing Christ with someone, what is your starting point to connect?

The word evangelism means the spreading of the Christian gospel by public preaching and personal witness. We often view evangelism as a person's conversion, the particular moment of decision to accept Christ. However, if evangelism is a process that leads to conversion, what is the most effective way to evangelize?

Putting things into context, how might these be good questions?

Where is the person I'm genuinely friends with as far as what he/she believes about life and God?

What does he/she need to take their next step and how does that give me a starting point?

When we consider evangelism from the other person's perspective, we discover people are at different places of interest and understanding. Discipleship evangelism is a process.

How might I properly share the gospel with someone who has no interest, who is curious, who is looking for answers, who is ready to commit?

A person: (1) with no interest	(2) who is curious	(3) looking for answers	(4) ready to commit
What they say: "It's good for you but not for me"	"I don't see the need"	"There must be more to this life"	"Jesus Christ is Lord, I repent of my sin and receive Christ"
What can I do?: Become a friend	Let my light shine	Share my conversion story	Romans 10:13
People don't care how much you know, until they know how much you care.	1 Peter 3:15 (presence)	Romans 10:14; 17 (proclamation)	Matthew 28:19-20 Discipling people to Jesus and on to maturity.

Who can you connect with to share Christ and at what starting point?

Suggested Reading:
Life-Style Evangelism, Joseph C. Aldrich
The Master Plan of Evangelism, Robert E. Coleman

Watch a training video for disciple makers about this coaching tool.
www.relevantministry.org/relevantdiscipleship

EVANGELISM

lessons

Instructions:

Relevant Discipleship™ may be launched in your ministry or church in a variety of ways. A primary way is with the Train the Discipler™ Workshop. Following this three-hour workshop, use the 12 lessons in this section in your small groups or Sunday School classes. The lessons are shared to reinforce the one-to-one discipleship happening outside of the group or class. If you're not in a group or class, there are 7 of the 12 lessons noted with an asterisk (∗) in the listing on the next page to consider for your one-to-one discipleship sessions.

Suggested group or class flow for facilitators and teachers:

- Start as you normally begin your group or class. Then, when it's time for the lesson, use the 12 lessons in this section of the resource manual. Some lessons may have two parts, use your discretion as to how you would like to teach each lesson, as you lead your group or class.

- To cover these 12 discipleship lessons, you could potentially meet 12 to 20 times.

- During this time period, people in your group or class will be meeting one-to-one every two or three weeks sometime other than when the group or class meets.

- As you are learning the coaching approach techniques in your own one-to-one discipleship, consider how you might do some shifting to a coaching approach as you teach these lessons.

- Take some time for people to share their one-to-one discipleship experiences happening outside of your group or class.

- From time to time demonstrate and practice one-to-one discipleship in your group or class. These could be five minutes in length using the Nehemiah Response Coaching Model™.

Suggested one-to-one discipleship session flow for the disciple maker:

- Several days before you meet, confirm your session date, time, and place.

- Use the Nehemiah Response Coaching Model™ to help guide your conversation. Begin by asking, "Where would you like to start today?"

- Engage and ask questions about his/her experience around the discipline he/she chose to focus on for the past two or three weeks. "How did you see God show up?"

- Ask, "What thoughts did the devotional articles or coaching tool stimulate around the discipline you have been focusing on?"

- Work through the suggested (*) discipleship lesson, unless your disciplee is part of a group or class where the lessons are being taught.

- Ask, "What are your thoughts around the lesson and how might you apply this lesson to your life?"

- Pick the next discipline to focus on. Share that the other disciplines you have previously focused on will not be disregarded. The purpose behind the focus on one discipline is to learn and grow in that area during the two or three weeks. Ultimately, a growing disciple will experience a balance of all 7 disciplines at all times.

- Point out too, the disciplines are not a set of actions to check-off each day. Rather, practicing the disciplines are about making room to experience God.

Lessons: titles and descriptions

Lesson 1: *Being a disciple

With this lesson, you will learn what it means to count the cost of being a disciple. As you begin your discipleship pathway journey, Jesus' words will help you consider what it will take to be a disciple.

Lesson 2: *Subjective self evaluation

Do the subjective self evaluation lesson by thinking where you would place yourself right now on a scale of 1-10. This will give you the chance to reflect on and share your strengths and growth areas in each discipline. At the end of the six-month period, you will take another evaluation. Anticipate what God will be doing around each discipline and the stories you might be sharing at the end of your six-month journey.

Lesson 3: *The Relevant Discipleship Pathway™

As you begin experiencing the discipleship pathway, you will work through an important lesson titled, The Relevant Discipleship Pathway™. You will discover how Jesus interacted with his disciples during his three years of ministry. Imagine if you were a disciple then, you'd have the same choices to make that you're making now as a follower of Christ.

Lesson 4: *What's your conversion story?

You'll have a chance to share your conversion story with each other. Your story, of how Jesus Christ gave you eternal life, is a powerful way of sharing your faith. Your story is unique and reveals how God is at work in showing his love to everyone.

Lesson 5: Write your conversion story

The next step is to write out your conversion story. Writing will help you develop a clear, concise personal conversion story. It will prepare you to share as God gives you opportunities to share your story.

Lesson 6: The 7 disciplines of a disciple in Acts and Revelation

Rationale for the 7 disciplines is that they connect with the seven churches written about in the last book of the Bible. With this lesson, you'll take a deeper look at the 7 disciplines of a disciple by making the connection of each one of the disciplines with the DNA of the early church in Acts and with the seven churches of Revelation.

Lesson 7: *Nehemiah Response Coaching Model™
At this point, on the discipleship pathway, we want to lift up the value of coaching. The Relevant Discipleship Pathway™ uses a 'coaching approach' and this is the coaching model we use. Think about how you have already experienced a coaching approach in your one-to-one discipleship sessions. Also, be thinking about the possibility of coaching yourself in your daily walk with God.

Lesson 8: How is God at work in your life?
This lesson consists of a number of short statements describing Relevant Discipleship™. They are actual 'tweets' posted on Twitter @nelsonroth. At this point on the discipleship pathway, which of these statements speak the loudest to you? Look the statements or 'tweets' over, and be ready to share what's meaningful to you about discipleship.

Lesson 9: *What does the Bible teach about the Holy Spirit?
In John's account of the Great Commission in chapter 20, Jesus says, "I am sending you." Then, he "breathed on them and said to them, Receive the Holy Spirit." Around forty days later in Acts 1:8, the first-century disciples were promised, "... you will receive power when the Holy Spirit has come upon you, and you will be my witnesses in Jerusalem and in all Judea and Samaria, and to the end of the earth." As you work through this lesson, consider the importance of living a Spirit-filled life.

Lesson 10: Practice the Presence of God
Practice of the Presence of God is the name of a short classic book of letters written by Brother Lawrence over 300 years ago. You will be able to use this lesson daily to help with the habit of what Brother Lawrence calls, "the holy habit of thinking of Him often." Habits, like 'thinking of him often', are the outcomes of practicing the 7 disciplines.

Lesson 11: *The 7 disciplines - Outcomes self evaluation
You have focused on all 7 disciplines over the past six months! As you look back on your journey, what are the ways God has worked in your life? In this self evaluation there are five possible outcomes listed under each of the 7 disciplines. These outcomes are real contributions from others at the end of their first six months of one-to-one discipleship. There's also a blank under each discipline to write something in particular you now notice in your life.

Lesson 12: One way I will intentionally practice each discipline
You've crossed the finish line! But, it's not over. As you continue your discipleship journey, what would happen for you around personal transformation and discipleship multiplication, if with each six-month discipleship cycle you intentionally chose a particular way to practice each of the 7 disciplines? This lesson will help you put a plan together to keep you moving forward. Determine a particular practice for each discipline and check-in on your progress with someone from time to time.

If you begin one-to-one discipleship prior to attending a Train the Discipler™ Workshop, you will want to cover this introductory lesson, *Before you begin*. During the 40 to 50 minutes you have together, discuss the lesson, make plans to meet seven times over the next six months, and have the disciplee choose his/her first discipline focus.

Introduction to Relevant Discipleship™

"And he said to them, "Follow me, and I will make you fishers of men." Matthew 4:19

The following is the definition for Relevant Discipleship™:

Relevant Discipleship is an intentional, transformational process of multiplying devoted followers of Christ where God is central; the 3Rs are evidences of spiritual health, and the practice of the 7 disciplines make room to know and love God.

What words in this definition stand out to you?

How would this definition, if implemented, impact discipleship for you?

The Relevant Discipleship Pathway™ is a continuous process of a series of six-month periods.

1. Meeting seven times one-to-one for an intentional and transformational time around the 7 disciplines of a disciple. These sessions are two to three weeks apart.
2. At the conclusion of each session, you choose one of the 7 disciplines to focus on next.
3. There are articles, coaching tools, and lessons in this resource manual for each discipline.

What makes Relevant Discipleship™ unique?

It's the coaching approach to discipleship. The coaching approach facilitates a relational process that is intentional, transformational, and multiplying. As you experience Relevant Discipleship™ you will become familiar with The Nehemiah Response Coaching Model™.

On the Relevant Discipleship Pathway™, you'll experience relationships∗ with God and others; respond∗ to how God is at work, and discover opportunities to reveal∗ Christ in your life! (∗3Rs)

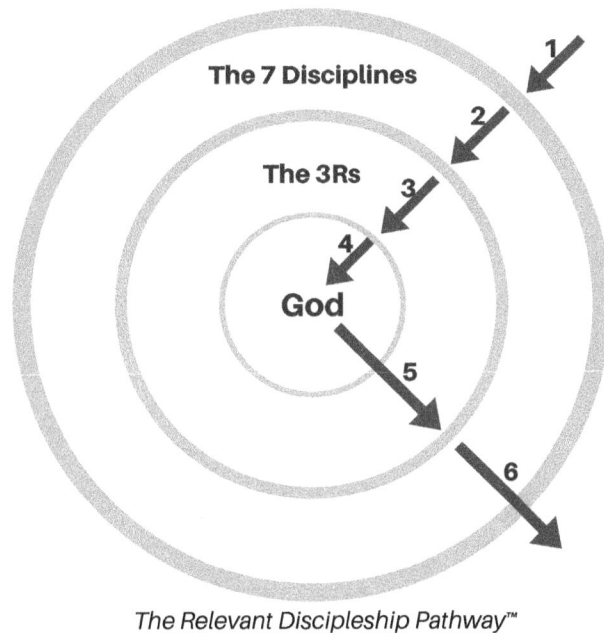

The Relevant Discipleship Pathway™

The 3Rs of The Relevant Discipleship Pathway™

The 3Rs come directly from the Greatest Commandment and the Great Commission of the New Testament. These core values are vital to Relevant Discipleship™ and are evidences of spiritual health in the life and ministry of a disciple; along with the 7 disciplines, Christ followers and their churches are transformed. Ministry that's relevant is:

- **Relational** – authentically seeking to (1)_____ and (2)_____ God
- **Responsive** – (3)_____ others by living life on mission and sharing the Gospel
- and, **Reveals Christ** – letting our '(4)_____ _____', incarnational living and walking in the Spirit

How would you like to see God at work in your life in these three areas?

Are you ready to get started?

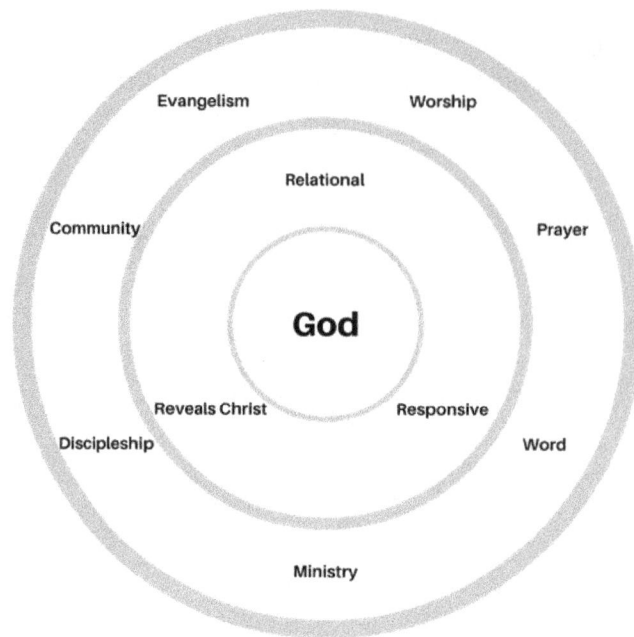

Relevant Discipleship™
The 3Rs and 7 disciplines

The 7 disciplines of a disciple, the daily practices of a Christ follower

The 7 disciplines of a disciple flow inward, making room to experience God. And then, flow outward from the center bringing transformation in our lives around the 3Rs. The 7 disciplines of a disciple come from the DNA of the New Testament church found in Acts 2:42-47 and also from the seven churches of Revelation.

The 7 disciplines:

- Worship - (5)_____ God when gathered with other believers and through the week as a lifestyle

- Prayer - (6)_____ with God alone and with others

- Word - developing a deep relationship with God and having passion to (7)_____ him more

- Ministry - discovering spiritual gifts and (8)_____ like Christ

- Discipleship - growing godly in (9)_____ with a foundation of personal values and purpose

- Community - loving one another and (10)_____ life

- Evangelism - cultivating intentional (11)_____ with not yet believers

During this six-month discipleship journey you will focus on one discipline for practice and growth between each one-to-one discipleship session. Which discipline would you like to choose to start your journey?

What do you hope to accomplish from your six-month journey?

Watch a training video for disciple makers for the Introductory one-to-one session.
www.relevantministry.org/relevantdiscipleship

The cost of being a disciple. Luke 14:25-33

- How do the two conditions of being a disciple at the beginning of this passage, in verses 26-27, challenge you?

- What's your understanding of the stories of building a tower, in verses 28-30, and a king going to war, in verses 31-32?

- What life changes might the third condition of being a disciple in verse 33 mean for you?

What is a disciple?

According to Vine's Expository Dictionary of New Testament Words, disciple means "one who follows another's teaching." When Jesus called Peter and Andrew, he said, *"Come, follow me,"* in Matthew 4:19.

The word "disciple" literally means a (1)_____ and a (2)_____ .

What will the outcome be for the believer who follows Christ?

The apostle Paul writes about God's goal in the redemption of mankind in Romans 8:29, *"For those God foreknew he also predestined to be conformed to the image of his Son."* Jesus said, in Luke 6:40, *"...everyone who is fully trained will be like their teacher."*

What will a believer's life begin to look like as they learn from and follow Jesus?

1. Disciples (3) _____ / _____ to Jesus' words. *"Jesus said, 'If you hold to my teaching, you are really my disciples."* John 8:31

2. Disciples (4) _____ each other. *"A new commandment I give to you, that you love one another: just as I have loved you, you also are to love one another. By this all people will know that you are my disciples, if you have love for one another."* John 13:34-35
    This is a love patterned after the love of Jesus (*"as I have loved you"* v. 34)
    This is a love that is visible to the world (*"by this all will know"* v. 35)

3. Disciples bear (5) _____ . *"By this my Father is glorified, that you bear much fruit and so prove to be my disciples."* John 15:8
    Jesus is not talking about an occasional good deed, rather a lifestyle which prompts people to glorify God! *"In the same way, let your light shine before others, so that they may see your good works and give glory to your Father who is in heaven."* Matthew 5:16

What will it take for you to be a disciple?

"Whoever wants to be my disciple must deny themselves and take up their cross daily and follow me." Luke 9:23

Discipleship is not (6)_____ **for the believer, it involves making right choices to continually learn and follow Christ.**

"In fact, though by this time you ought to be teachers, you need someone to teach you the elementary truths of God's word all over again. You need milk, not solid food! Anyone who lives on milk, being still an infant, is not acquainted with the teaching about righteousness." Hebrews 5:12-13

Discipleship is a process that takes (7)_____ **and**
(8)_____ **.**

"Grow (continue to, keep on growing) in the grace and knowledge of our Lord and Savior Jesus Christ. To him be glory both now and forever! Amen." 2 Peter 3:18

"...train yourself to be godly." 1 Timothy 4:7

What are the challenges to make Jesus first in your life?

What will be your response to the call to be a learner and follower of Christ?

Watch a training video for disciple makers about this lesson.
www.relevantministry.org/relevantdiscipleship

For each of the 7 disciplines, mark below - "Here's where I'm at right now," with 1 being the lowest and 10 being the highest. Ask yourself ... "How satisfied am I right now for each discipline as it relates to my current life experiences?"

Listed with each discipline is it's short description and it's Acts and Revelation reference:

WORSHIP – experiencing God when gathered with other believers and through the week as a lifestyle

"praising God" - Acts 2:47

Ephesus, *"forsaken their first love"* - Revelation 2:4

1---------2---------3---------4---------5---------6---------7---------8---------9---------10

PRAYER – communicating with God alone and with others

"They devoted themselves - to the breaking of bread and to prayer" - Acts 2:42

Smyrna, *"don't be afraid - the devil will put some of you in prison to test you - be faithful"* - Revelation 2:10

1---------2---------3---------4---------5---------6---------7---------8---------9---------10

WORD – developing a deep relationship with God and having passion to know him more

"They devoted themselves to the apostles' teaching" - Acts 2:42

Pergamos, *"compromised their faith and needed to repent"* - Revelation 2:16

1---------2---------3---------4---------5---------6---------7---------8---------9---------10

MINISTRY – discovering spiritual gifts and serving like Christ

"to give to anyone who had need" - Acts 2:45

Thyatira, *"loved the world and concerned about self"* - Revelation 2:20

1---------2---------3---------4---------5---------6---------7---------8---------9---------10

DISCIPLESHIP – growing godly in character with a foundation of personal values and purpose

"They devoted themselves" - Acts 2:42

Sardis, *"fallen asleep and just going through the motions"* - Revelation 3:2

1---------2---------3---------4---------5---------6---------7---------8---------9---------10

COMMUNITY – loving one another and sharing life

"They devoted themselves - to fellowship" - Acts 2:42

Philadelphia, *"had an open door"* - Revelation 3:8 (*philea* = brotherly love)

1---------2---------3---------4---------5---------6---------7---------8---------9---------10

EVANGELISM – cultivating intentional friendships with not yet believers

"enjoying the favor of all the people. And the Lord added to their number daily those who were being saved" - Acts 2:47

Laodecia, *"lukewarm - self-sufficient and inward focused"* - Revelation 3:16

1---------2---------3---------4---------5---------6---------7---------8---------9---------10

Over the next six months:

What growth in your spiritual walk would you like to see?

What challenges to overcome do you see standing in the way of your spiritual growth?

Watch a training video for disciple makers about this lesson.
www.relevantministry.org/relevantdiscipleship

The inward and outward journey of the Discipleship Pathway...

The 7 disciplines of a disciple flow inward, and when practiced, **makes room for us to experience God.** The Pathway then, flows outward from the center bringing transformation in our lives around the 3Rs - Relational, Responsive, Reveals Christ.

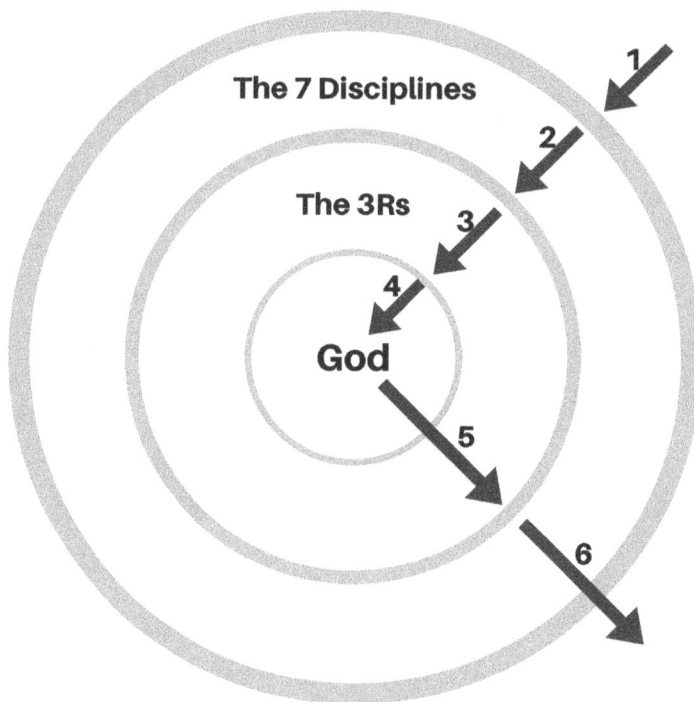

The Relevant Discipleship Pathway™

Training of the Twelve, A.B. Bruce, 1871
"The twelve arrived at their final intimate relation to Jesus only by degrees, three stages in the history of their fellowship with Him being distinguishable."

"The Relevant Discipleship Pathway is a descriptive way of understanding how each person is invited to move from viewing faith to abiding in God's presence. And yet, that's not the final chapter. The path leads us into the presence of God, transforms and sends us."

Missiologist and Theological educator, Kansas

Here is the chronological timeline of how Jesus interacted with his disciples after his baptism:

1. "Come and (1)_____ " - John 1:35-46 ((2)_____ months)

2. "Come, (3)_____ me" - Mark 1:16-20 ((4)_____months)

3. "He appointed twelve that they might (5)_____ _____him" - Mark 3:13-14 ((6)_____ months)

4. "(7)_____in me and I in you" - John 15:5-8 (final instructions before the cross)

5. "Everyone ... fully trained will be like their teacher" - Luke 6:40 (transformation, (8)_____ years)

6. "Let your (9)_____ _____ before others" - Matthew 5:14-16 (10)_____ years)

How does seeing the timeline of this pathway impact you as a Christ follower?

Who could you ask to join you in a journey like this?

Suggested 11-week Group Study:
Relevant Discipleship Pathway: a framework for intentional transformation that multiplies, Nelson Roth

Watch a training video for disciple makers about this lesson.
www.relevantministry.org/relevantdiscipleship

What's your conversion story?

1 The story of your response to God's call for salvation is important!

1. People are (1)_____ in stories.

2. People can (2)_____ to your story.

3. It is hard to (3)_____ with a true story.

Your story is (4)_____ and it is (5)_____.

Your story has the power to (6)_____ Christ to others.

"In the beginning was the Word..." (John 1:1). *"The Word (Jesus)*

became (7)_____ and made his dwelling among us"

(John 1:14).

2 In Acts 26:4–23, Paul tells his conversion story in three parts. Then in verse 27, he asks King Agrippa a most compelling question ... *"King Agrippa, do you believe?"*

Before Christ	**† - Conversion**	**After Conversion**
Paul describes his life growing up. He was a Pharisee, and he was convinced he should do everything possible to oppose the teachings of Jesus, including putting Christians in prison and even condemning them to death.	Paul relates how he came to Christ. Paul tells how he was on his way to Damascus to persecute Christians, when Christ appeared to him and appointed him to be a servant and a spokesman for Christ.	Paul shares his testimony about coming to Christ and preaches that people should repent, turn to God, and prove their repentance by their deeds.
Vs. 4 - 11	**Vs. 12 - 18**	**Vs. 19 -23**

3   Make notes about your life Before Christ, Your Conversion, and After Conversion

Before Christ

---

† - Conversion

After Conversion

With whom could you share your conversion story?

Adapted from, *Becoming a Contagious Christian* by Bill Hybels and Mark Mittleberg

Watch a training video for disciple makers about this lesson.
www.relevantministry.org/relevantdiscipleship

Writing your conversion story can help clarify what to share with family, friends, and people you know. **How would your conversion story be helpful to them?**

"'Return home and tell how much God has done for you.' So, the man went away and told all over town how much Jesus had done for him." Luke 8:39

Consider these things as you develop your story:

1. **Theme** – What is a central topic that shows the contrast in your spiritual outlook before and after knowing Christ?

2. **Conclusion** – What is a question you could ask, after you share your story, that requires a response?

3. **Scripture** – What was one key Bible verse that opened your eyes?

4. **Language** – Be real when you share. Avoid Christian clichés and "God-talk."

5. **Length** – Be brief, to the point and laser focused when you share.

6. **Putting others first** – When telling your story, keep your focus on your friend. Emphasize those aspects of your story that will relate to their concerns and interests.

7. **Allow the Spirit to lead** – *"No one can come to me unless the Father who sent me draws them."* John 6:44

From your notes in lesson 4, further develop your conversion story by answering the following questions.

Your life before Christ

1   **Where were you spiritually before receiving Christ, and how did that affect you - your feelings, attitudes, actions, and relationships?**

2   **What caused you to begin considering Christ as the solution to your need?**

† - Conversion, how you met Jesus Christ

3   When you realized you needed Christ in your life, what motivated you to accept Christ?

4   Specifically, how did you receive Christ?

After conversion, how your life has changed

5   How did your life begin to change after you trusted Christ? (Contrast your life with what it might have been like without Christ.)

6   What other benefits have you experienced since becoming a Christian?

Who could you partner with to practice telling your story in three minutes?

Adapted from, *Becoming a Contagious Christian* by Bill Hybels and Mark Mittleberg

Suggested Relevant Ministry Workshop:
Ask your Relevant Discipleship Coach about hosting the **Your Life Story Workshop** at your church. Your conversion story is part of your life story. Participants of this workshop consider God's working throughout their entire life journey. New insights from this workshop reveal God's plan and empowers you for the future.

There are seven evidences of spiritual health for life and ministry found in the early church in
(1)_____ and mostly non existent in the seven churches of (2)_____ .
These seven evidences are the 7 (3)_____ of a disciple.

The 7 disciplines are in the DNA of the early church found in Acts 2:42-47. They are also found
in the seven churches of Revelation by either what Christ commended or warned about as he
evaluated those churches.

The 7 disciplines of a disciple in Acts 2:

Acts 2:42-47, " [42] *They devoted themselves to the apostles' teaching and to fellowship, to the
breaking of bread and to prayer.* [43] *Everyone was filled with awe at the many wonders and signs
performed by the apostles.* [44] *All the believers were together and had everything in common.*
[45] *They sold property and possessions to give to anyone who had need.* [46] *Every day they
continued to meet together in the temple courts. They broke bread in their homes and ate
together with glad and sincere hearts,* [47] *praising God and enjoying the favor of all the people.
And the Lord added to their number daily those who were being saved.*"

Worship	*"praising God"* - Acts 2:47
Prayer	*"They devoted themselves...to the breaking of bread and to prayer"* - Acts 2:42
Word	*"They devoted themselves to the apostles' teaching"* - Acts 2:42
Ministry	*"to give to anyone who had need"* - Acts 2:45
Discipleship	*"They devoted themselves"* - Acts 2:42
Community	*"They devoted themselves...to fellowship"* - Acts 2:42
Evangelism	*"enjoying the favor of all the people. And the Lord added to their number daily those who were being saved"* - Acts 2:47

The 7 disciplines of a disciple in Revelation 2-3:

Worship   Ephesus, *"forsaken their first (4)_____"* - Revelation 2:4

Prayer   Smyrna, *"don't be afraid - the devil will put some of you in prison to test you - be (5)_____"* - Revelation 2:10

Word   Pergamos, *"compromised their (6)_____ and needed to repent"* - Revelation 2:16

Ministry   Thyatira, *"loved the world and concerned about (7)_____"* - Revelation 2:20

Discipleship Sardis, *"fallen asleep and just going through the (8)_____"* - Revelation 3:2

Community   Philadelphia, *"had an (9)_____ door"* - Revelation 3:8 (philea = brotherly love)

Evangelism   Laodecia, *"lukewarm - self-sufficient and (10)_____ focused"* - Revelation 3:16

Where is the church now regarding these seven evidences of spiritual health? Or, possibly the better question is, since people are the church, where are you right now regarding these seven evidences of spiritual health in your life?

How could a journey of following Christ around the 7 disciplines of a disciple impact your life and ministry?

Suggested Reading:
What is the church to be? by Nelson Roth
The 7 marks of a healthy church by Nelson Roth

The Nehemiah Response Coaching Model™ is a biblical, transitional process for revitalization and transformation. The model helps guide the conversation during your one-to-one discipleship sessions.

The Nehemiah Response Coaching Model™ captures responses of Nehemiah and will help to develop **a custom solution to get from where you are** (Present Situation) **to where you want to go** (Preferred Future). The metaphor is a circle rolling forward along a line to your Preferred Future from your Present Situation.

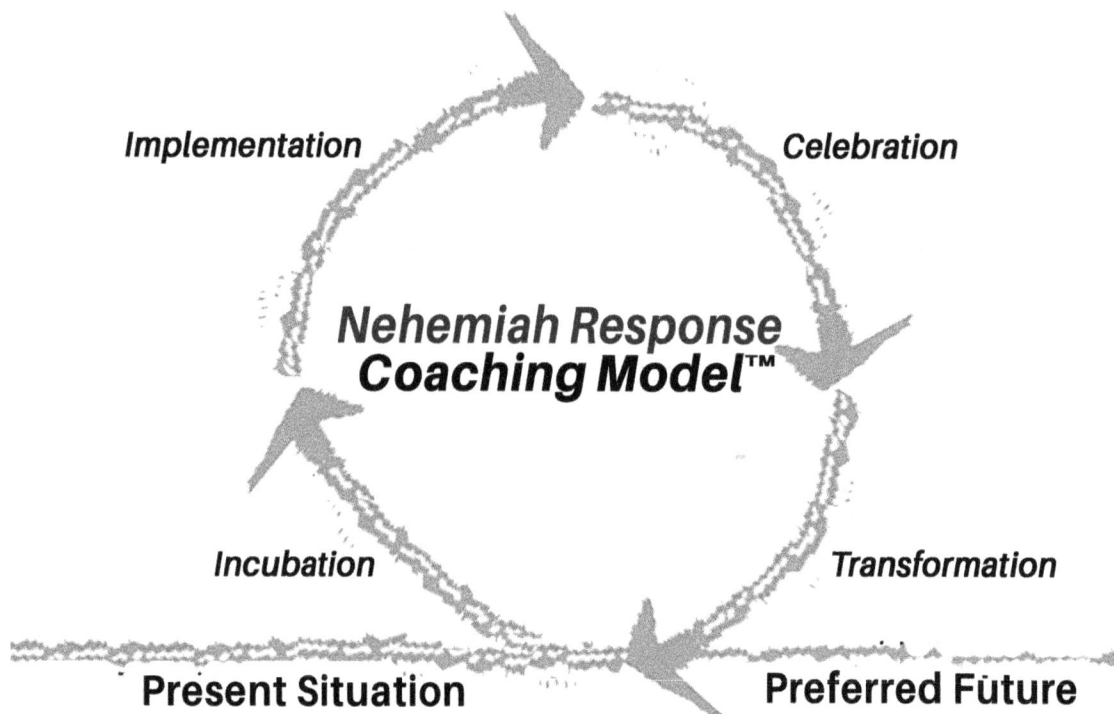

Implementation   *Celebration*

Nehemiah Response
***Coaching Model*™**

Incubation   *Transformation*

Present Situation   **Preferred Future**

If I mentor you the tendency is for you to become like me,
Relevant Discipleship takes a coaching approach where we both
become like Christ. @nelsonroth

The Relevant Discipleship coaching approach works providing the
support most people need to form new habits. @nelsonroth

Possible questions to ask:

Preferred Future

Present Situation

Incubation

Implementation

Celebration

Transformation

Suggested 11-week Group Study:
Nehemiah Response: a coaching model, Nelson and Pam Roth

Watch a training video for disciple makers about this lesson.
www.relevantministry.org/relevantdiscipleship

How is God at work in your life?

What statements speak the loudest to you? Check the boxes below.

☐ 1 *Discipleship is a transformational process that takes time. It challenges our consumer mentality that 'the next big event' is our solution.*

☐ 2 *The disciplines become evidences of spiritual health in life and ministry. They make room for Christ to work from the inside out.*

☐ 3 *A spiritual journey that integrates Relevant Discipleship helps you discover your mission in the world.*

☐ 4 *Being a disciple takes us beyond our level of comfort where the only thing we can do is depend on God.*

☐ 5 *Discipleship is about becoming like Christ. We do that by the indwelling Spirit not by our doing. Relevant Discipleship is about abiding.*

☐ 6 *Discipleship is following Christ on his terms not ours. What changes does that mean for you?*

☐ 7 *When Christian leadership and ministry responsibility precedes discipleship, burn-out and bail-out down the road is more likely to occur.*

☐ 8 *If I mentor you the tendency is for you to become like me. Relevant Discipleship takes a coaching approach where we both become like Christ.*

☐ 9 *The question to ask around the 7 disciplines is not, "Can I check it off for today?" Rather, "How did my activity bring me closer to God?"*

☐ 10 *Relevant Discipleship's 7 disciplines of a disciple are more about our inward connection and encountering God than our outward activity.*

☐ 11 *Relevant Discipleship takes a coaching approach that helps you grow in life and your relationship with God.*

☐ 12 *What would a discipleship process that multiplies disciples integrated into the life of your church look like?*

☐ 13 *The 7 disciplines of Relevant Discipleship are interrelated, development in one discipline has positive impact on the others.*

☐ 14 *The spiritual discipline you're practicing at a particular time does not transform you, it makes room for a deeper relationship with God.*

☐ 15 *Relevant Discipleship is less about a training program and more about how to become like Jesus.*

☐ 16 *Relevant Discipleship is a judgement free safe place where two people get real with each other and the Holy Spirit works.*

☐ 17 Discipleship is discipline. It's a lifestyle that requires a cross. What does your journey of following look like?

☐ 18 Disciples making disciples, a transformational process of multiplying devoted followers of Christ. That's the goal of the Relevant Discipleship Pathway.

☐ 19 Relevant Discipleship leaves the classroom and through relationships and practical application reveals Christ in your life.

☐ 20 Relevant Discipleship is about becoming like Jesus, not just learning about Jesus. Ready to start?

☐ 21 Where do you see a discipleship deficiency? What's your plan, if disciples making disciples is your desire?

☐ 22 The coaching approach to discipleship helps you multiply your experience with others.

☐ 23 Relevant Discipleship is a transformational process where God is central with the 3Rs at its core.

☐ 24 Christ followers were called disciples. Later, disciples were called Christians in the book of Acts. What's missing today?

☐ 25 One-to-one discipleship works. God created us for mutual interdependence. "Iron sharpens iron" Proverbs 27:17

☐ 26 Discipleship is a process not a program. If that's true, how does it change the way you experience discipleship?

Why did the statements you checked speak to you?

From the statements you checked, which one or two statements would you pick to describe what being a disciple means to you right now?

What actions will you take based on the statements you picked?

Based on these actions, what are the personal outcomes you hope to see over the next several months?

There are three word designations in the New Testament about the believer's relationship with the Holy Spirit that are important to understand. We will consider all three in this lesson.

(1) _____ (2) _____ (3) _____

Just before his death and resurrection, Jesus taught his disciples about the (4)_____ of the Holy Spirit. John 14:15-17; 25-26

Thirty years later, Paul said this in 1 Corinthians 6:19-20, "your body is a temple of the Holy Spirit (5)_____ you."

Today, as disciples and followers of Christ, the inclusion of the Holy Spirit in our walk is essential.

① Who is the Holy Spirit?

He is the (6)_____ person of the Trinity. 2 Corinthians 13:14, *"The grace of the Lord Jesus Christ and the love of God and the fellowship of the Holy Spirit be with you all."*

> The Holy Spirit is not a shadow or an impersonal force. He is a person, equal in every way with the Father and the Son, Jesus Christ. All of the divine attributes are ascribed to the Holy Spirit. The Father, Son, and Spirit are one; and yet, they each have distinct roles.

② The Holy Spirit in the Old Testament: (Old Covenant)

The Holy Spirit, like God, has (7)_____ since the beginning. Genesis 1:1-2, *"In the beginning God created the heavens and the earth...and the Spirit of God was hovering over the waters."*

The Holy Spirit was active in the Old Testament as he came (8)_____certain people at different times for specific purposes to serve God.

> Pharaoh, for example, said this about Joseph, *"Can we find anyone like this man, one in whom is the Spirit of God?"* Genesis 41:38. And, David said in 2 Samuel 23:2, *"The Spirit of the Lord spoke through me; his word was on my tongue."* When Jesus began his ministry in John 1:32-33, John the Baptist said, *"I saw the Spirit descend from heaven like a dove, and it remained on him ... he who sent me to baptize with water said to me, 'He on whom you see the Spirit descend and remain, this is he who baptizes with the Holy Spirit.'"*

③ The Holy Spirit in the New Testament: (New Covenant)

The Spirit's first work in the lives of all people.

Since the resurrection of Jesus, the Holy Spirit's initial role in the lives of people is to make them aware of their need for (9)_____.

> *"When he comes, he will convict the world of guilt in regard to sin and righteousness and judgment..."* John 16:8

The Spirit's work in the life of the believer.

Today, when a person accepts Jesus Christ as their Lord and Savior; they are (10)_____ with the Holy Spirit.

- Romans 8:9, *"...if anyone does not have the Spirit of Christ, he does not belong to Christ."*
- Galatians 4:6, *"Because you are sons, God sent the Spirit of his Son into our hearts"*
- I Corinthians 6:19, *"Do you not know that your body is the temple of the Holy Spirit."*

Since the (11)_____ of Christ, when a person receives Christ, the Holy Spirit immediately indwells the believer.

- John 7:37-39, *"Up to that time the Spirit had not been given..."* [(12)_____ resurrection]
- John 14:17, *"...for he lives with you, and will be in you."* [(13)_____ resurrection]
- John 20:22, *"...He breathed on them and said, 'Receive the Holy Spirit'."* [(14 _____ resurrection]

It's possible for a believer to be indwelt but not baptized or (15)_____ with the Spirit.

- Acts 1:5, *"...(Jesus) for John baptized with water, but you will be baptized with the Holy Spirit not many days from now."*
- Acts 1:8, *"...you will receive power when the Holy Spirit comes on you."*
- Acts 2:4, *"And they were all filled with the Holy Spirit."* (there is an initial Spirit baptism or filling)
- Ephesians 5:18, *"...Be filled with the Spirit."* (filled - (v.) present tense, continuous and imperative)

We live the spirit filled life in order to (16) _____ in the Spirit.

- Galatians 5:16, tells us to *"live by (walk in) the Spirit."*

As a believer, you (17)_____all of the Holy Spirit. An important question to ask ...
Does the Holy Spirit (18)_____all of me?

The understanding of three different word designations are important in the believer's relationship with the Holy Spirit. Believers are (19)_____ immediately at their salvation, they are to be (20)_____with the Spirit; which can happen at salvation, or sometime later, and they are to continue to be filled and (21)_____ in the Spirit; living a godly life and serving effectively!

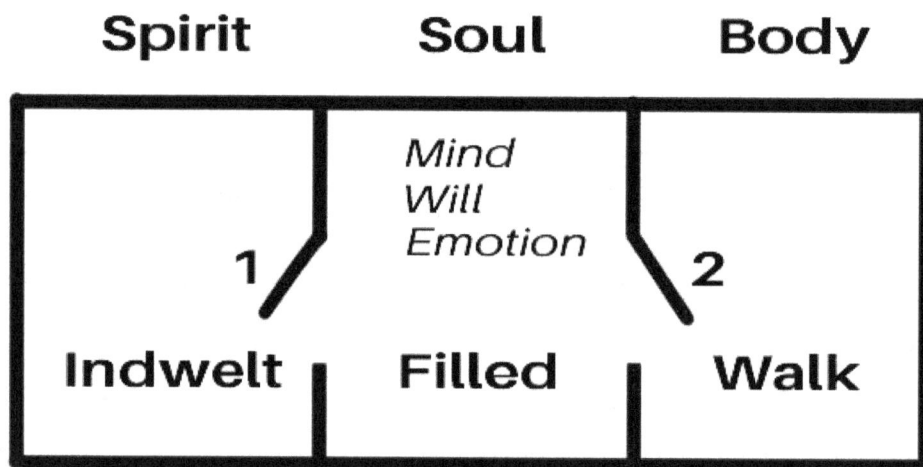

Spirit   Soul   Body

Spirit	Soul	Body
	Mind Will Emotion	
1		2
Indwelt	**Filled**	**Walk**

"May God himself, the God of peace, sanctify you through and through.
May your whole spirit, soul and body be kept blameless at the
coming of our Lord Jesus Christ."
1 Thessalonians 5:23

In review:

From the day of their salvation, a believer is (22)_____with the Holy Spirit.

Being filled with the Spirit can happen at salvation; however, it is a (23)_____ transaction.

There is a difference in the Spirit being (24)_____ _____ and the Spirit being (25)_____ _____

As believers, we're to (26)_____ "be filled with the Spirit."

As a believer, you have (27)_____ of the Holy Spirit but, does he have (28)_____ of you?

The baptism of the Spirit or being filled with the Spirit is God's promise and gift. He is the giver and we are the receiver by yielding to the Holy Spirit's indwelling presence. Luke 11:13, "How much more will your (29)_____in heaven give the Holy Spirit to those who ask!"

The purpose for the presence and power of the Spirit in the believer's life is found in Acts 1:8, "But you will receive power when the Holy Spirit comes on you; and you will be my witnesses in Jerusalem, and in all Judea and Samaria, and to the ends of the earth."

If you are a believer, the Holy Spirit is 'in you'.

What action is the Spirit of God prompting you to take now?

Suggested Reading:
The Release of The Spirit, Watchman Nee
Have you Made the Wonderful Discovery of the Spirit-Filled Life, Bill Bright
Joy Unspeakable: Power and Renewal in the Holy Spirit, Martyn Lloyd-Jones

Watch a training video for disciple makers about this lesson.
www.relevantministry.org/relevantdiscipleship

The Practice of the Presence of God, by Brother Lawrence

Brother Lawrence was a kitchen worker in a monastery in Paris over 300 years ago. The monks actually looked to him because of his spirituality. *The Practice of the Presence of God* is a short classic book of letters written by Brother Lawrence compiled after his death.

Here's an excerpt from one letter:

*To be with Him, we must cultivate **the holy habit of thinking of Him often.** You will tell me that I always say the same thing. What can I say? It is true. I don't know an easier method, nor do I practice any other, so I advise this one to everybody. We have to know someone before we can truly love them. In order to know God, we must think about Him often. And once we get to know Him, we will think about Him even more often, because where our treasure is, there also is our heart!*
(Ninth Letter, p. 48)

The spiritual discipline you're practicing at a particular time does not transform you, it makes room for a deeper relationship with God. @nelsonroth

The 7 disciplines of Relevant Discipleship are interrelated, development in one has positive impact on the others. @nelsonroth

Suggested daily practice of the 7 disciplines:

As the Lord leads, read the three steps on the next page at the start of the day.

Then, at the end of the day, evaluate your experiences from practicing the disciplines through self coaching using the same steps along with powerful questions of the Nehemiah Response Coaching Model™.

Begin and end each day with the following reflections:

1. Who will be/was in the center of my life, and how will/did I make room today to know and love God?

2. How am I being transformed around the 3Rs?
    Being Relational
    (head)
    Being Responsive
    (hands and feet, missional)
    Revealing Christ
    (heart, incarnational)

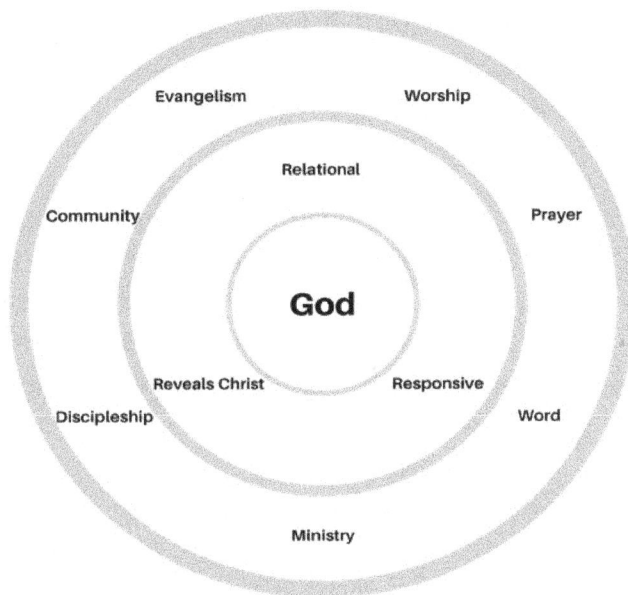

Relevant Discipleship™
The 3Rs and 7 disciplines

3. How will/was my daily practice of the 7 disciplines be integrated into my life today?

The 7 disciplines and their descriptions:	
Worship	experiencing God when gathered with other believers and through the week as a lifestyle
Prayer	communicating with God alone and with others
Word	developing a deep relationship with God and having passion to know him more
Ministry	discovering spiritual gifts and serving like Christ
Discipleship	growing godly in character with a foundation of personal values and purpose
Community	loving one another and sharing life
Evangelism	cultivating intentional friendships with not yet believers

Outcomes self evaluation

This is a reflective tool, to evaluate outcomes from the past six months of your ongoing discipleship journey. It will help you evaluate spiritual strengths and current areas for spiritual growth as you continue your journey.

Below are five outcome statements about each of the 7 disciplines. Check the ones that you now see evidenced in your life. These outcomes are real contributions from others at the end of their first six months of one-to-one discipleship. There's a blank under each discipline to write something in particular you now notice in your life.

WORSHIP – experiencing God when gathered with other believers and through the week as a lifestyle

"praising God" - Acts 2:47

Ephesus, *"forsaken their first love"* - Revelation 2:4

____ Worship is my response, both personally and corporately, to God for who he is.

____ I understand the importance of gathering regularly for worship and teaching.

____ I understand I exist for God's purposes and glory.

____ How I live my life daily shows I love God with all my heart.

____ God has first place and is in the center of my life.

____ _____

PRAYER – communicating with God alone and with others

"They devoted themselves - to the breaking of bread and to prayer" - Acts 2:42

Smyrna, *"don't be afraid - the devil will put some of you in prison to test you - be faithful"* - Revelation 2:10

____ I understand and use different forms of prayer: adoration, confession, thanksgiving.

____ I turn to God in spontaneous prayer throughout the day.

____ I regularly join in with others for prayer.

____ Since prayer is communication, I take time to be silent and listen to what God has to say.

____ I practice the habit of intercessory prayer, praying for others.

____ _____

WORD – developing a deep relationship with God and having passion to know him more

"They devoted themselves to the apostles' teaching" - Acts 2:42

Pergamos, *"compromised their faith and needed to repent"* - Revelation 2:16

____ I believe the Bible is the Word of God and is the authority in my life.

____ I consistently pursue the habit of reading the Bible to help me become more like Jesus.

____ When life changes or issues arise, I make decisions based on biblical principles.

____ I actively memorize and dedicate time to reflective meditation on God's Word.

____ My Bible reading and study has deepened my faith in God.

____ _____

MINISTRY – discovering spiritual gifts and serving like Christ

"to give to anyone who had need" - Acts 2:45

Thyatira, *"loved the world and concerned about self"* - Revelation 2:20

____ I know my spiritual gifts and use those gifts in ministry for the benefit of others.

____ I enjoy meeting the needs of others without expecting anything in return.

____ In serving, I strive to love as Jesus loved, and serve as Jesus served.

____ I look for new ways to serve and be missional where I live and work.

____ I know and align with the mission and vision of the church I affiliate with.

____ _____

DISCIPLESHIP – growing godly in character with a foundation of personal values and purpose

"They devoted themselves" - Acts 2:42

Sardis, *"fallen asleep and just going through the motions"* - Revelation 3:2

____ I understand the cost of being a disciple of Christ and am willing to die to self.

____ I am a committed follower of Christ, practicing the disciplines to make room for God.

____ Because it matters more "who I am," than "what I do," I am passionate about Christlikeness.

____ I am able to share a clear testimony of my conversion and how I came to Christ.

____ Since I've been discipled, I will engage in making disciples and the discipleship process.

____ _____

COMMUNITY – loving one another and sharing life

"They devoted themselves - to fellowship" - Acts 2:42

Philadelphia, *"had an open door"* - Revelation 3:8 (*philea* = brotherly love)

____ I am deepening my understanding of genuine relationships by fellowshipping with others.

____ I live out the relational instructions of the "one anothers" in the Bible.

____ When there is interpersonal conflict, I deal with it in a biblical manner.

____ I gather regularly in a small group for the purpose of growing spiritually and serving.

____ I meet regularly with someone for accountability and ongoing discipleship.

____ _____

EVANGELISM – cultivating intentional friendships with not yet believers

"enjoying the favor of all the people. And the Lord added to their number daily those who were being saved" - Acts 2:47

Laodecia, *"lukewarm - self-sufficient and inward focused"* - Revelation 3:16

____ I understand and am obedient to the Great Commission of going and making disciples.

____ I develop friendships with not yet believers for the purpose of being salt and light.

____ I understand the Gospel, who Jesus Christ is and what he has done for sinful mankind.

____ I desire and work at having an impact and positive influence in my community.

____ I am eager when given opportunity to share my conversion story.

____ _____

Where do you see personal growth and transformation over the past six months? Write your story below.

Would you consider sharing your discipleship experience, so we could share your story with others? Share with us at
www.relevantministry.org/share.

Watch a training video for disciple makers about this lesson.
www.relevantministry.org/relevantdiscipleship

Now, that you've experienced the Relevant Discipleship Pathway™ the past six months, how would your personal transformation and disciple making be impacted if every six months you intentionally chose one way to practice each of the 7 disciplines? And for encouragement and help, who can you check-in with on your progress from time to time?

In the boxes below, write out a particular way you will intentionally practice each discipline for the next six months.

WORSHIP – experiencing God when gathered with other believers and through the week as a lifestyle

"praising God" - Acts 2:47

Ephesus, *"forsaken their first love"* - Revelation 2:4

PRAYER – communicating with God alone and with others

"They devoted themselves - to the breaking of bread and to prayer" - Acts 2:42

Smyrna, *"don't be afraid - the devil will put some of you in prison to test you - be faithful"* - Revelation 2:10

WORD – developing a deep relationship with God and having passion to know him more

"They devoted themselves to the apostles' teaching" - Acts 2:42

Pergamos, *"compromised their faith and needed to repent"* - Revelation 2:16

DISCIPLESHIP – growing godly in character with a foundation of personal values and purpose

"They devoted themselves" - Acts 2:42

Sardis, *"fallen asleep and just going through the motions"* - Revelation 3:2

MINISTRY – discovering spiritual gifts and serving like Christ

"to give to anyone who had need" - Acts 2:45

Thyatira, *"loved the world and concerned about self"* - Revelation 2:20

COMMUNITY – loving one another and sharing life

"They devoted themselves - to fellowship" - Acts 2:42

Philadelphia, *"had an open door"* - Revelation 3:8 (*philea* = brotherly love)

EVANGELISM – cultivating intentional friendships with not yet believers

"enjoying the favor of all the people. And the Lord added to their number daily those who were being saved" - Acts 2:47

How do you feel about this statement? "Discipleship is a way of life for the rest of your life."

Who will you check-in with on how your practice of the disciplines is going?

As you continue your discipleship journey, what is your desire for personal transformation and disciple making?

bibliography

David Augsburger, *Dissident Discipleship: A Spirituality of Self-Surrender, Love of God, and Love of Neighbor*

George Barna, *Growing True Disciples: New Strategies for Producing Genuine Followers of Christ*

Dietrich Bonhoeffer, *The Cost of Discipleship*

Mike Breen and Steve Cockram, *Building a Discipleship Culture*

A.B. Bruce, *The Training of the Twelve*

Robert Coleman, *The Master Plan of Evangelism*

Leroy Eims, *The Lost Art of Disciple Making*

Richard Foster, *Celebration of Discipline: The Path to Spiritual Growth*

Richard Foster and Gayle Beebe, *Longing for God: Seven Paths of Christian Devotion*

Alan Hirsch and Debra Hirsch, *Untamed: Reactivating a Missional Form of Discipleship*

Bill Hull, *The Complete Book of Discipleship, on Being and Making Followers of Christ*

Gordon MacDonald, *Ordering Your Private World*

Aubrey Malphurs, *Strategic Disciple Making: A Practical Tool for Successful Ministry*

Henri Nouwen, *The Way of the Heart*

Henri Nouwen, *A Spirituality of Living*

Greg Ogden, *Transforming Discipleship: Making Disciples a Few at a Time*

J.I. Packer, *Knowing God*

Francis Schaeffer, *The Mark of a Christian*

Ray Stedman, *Authentic Christianity*

John Stott, *The Radical Disciple: Some Neglected Aspects of Our Calling*

Leonard Sweet, *I Am a Follower*

Dallas Willard, *Renovation of the Heart: Putting on the Character of Christ*

Dallas Willard, *The Spirit of the Disciplines: Understanding How God Changes Lives*

appendix

Before you begin, pages 90-93

1. know
2. love
3. loving
4. light shine
5. experiencing
6. communicating
7. know
8. serving
9. character
10. sharing
11. friendships

1. Being a disciple, pages 94-95

1. learner
2. follower
3. abide / hold
4. love
5. fruit
6. automatic
7. time
8. discipline

3. The Relevant Discipleship Pathway™, pages 98-99

1. see
2. 4-5
3. follow
4. 10-11
5. be with
6. 20
7. remain / abide
8. 2
9. light shine
10. 2

4. What's your conversion story, pages 100-101

1. interested
2. relate
3. argue / disagree
4. real / unique
5. powerful
6. reveal
7. flesh

6. The 7 disciplines of a disciple, pages 104-105

1. Acts
2. Revelation
3. disciplines
4. love
5. faithful
6. faith
7. self
8. motions
9. open
10. inward

9. What does the Bible teach about the Holy Spirit, pages 110-113

1. indwelt
2. baptized, filled, total surrender
3. walk
4. promise
5. within
6. third
7. existed
8. upon
9. salvation
10. indwelt
11. resurrection

12. pre

13. pre

14. post

15. filled

16. walk

17. have

18. have

19. indwelt

20. baptized or filled

21. walk

22. indwelt

23. separate

24. in you

25. on you

26. continually

27. all

28. all

29. Father

Disciplee's Name _____

Date _____

Introductory Session (Covered in the Train the Discipler™ Workshop)

_____ Lesson: Before you begin (p. 90-93)

_____ Discipline Articles for next session _____

_____ Discipline Coaching Tool for next session _____

Before each session, review the suggested session flow on pages 6 and 7.

① Date _____

First Discipleship Session

_____ Discipline Articles for next session _____

_____ Discipline Coaching Tool for next session _____

_____ Lesson 1: Being a disciple

② Date _____

Second Discipleship Session

_____ Discipline Articles for next session _____

_____ Discipline Coaching Tool for next session _____

_____ Lesson 2: Subjective self evaluation

③ Date _____

Third Discipleship Session

_____ Discipline Articles for next session _____

_____ Discipline Coaching Tool for next session _____

_____ Lesson 3: The Relevant Discipleship Pathway™

4 Date _____

Fourth Discipleship Session

_____ Discipline Articles for next session _____

_____ Discipline Coaching Tool for next session _____

_____ Lesson 4: What's your conversion story?

5 Date _____

Fifth Discipleship Session

_____ Discipline Articles for next session _____

_____ Discipline Coaching Tool for next session _____

_____ Lesson 7: The Nehemiah Response Coaching Model™

6 Date _____

Sixth Discipleship Session

_____ Discipline Articles for next session _____

_____ Discipline Coaching Tool for next session _____

_____ Lesson 9: What does the Bible teach about the Holy Spirit?

7 Date _____

Seventh Discipleship Session

_____ Lesson 11: Outcomes self evaluation

Nehemiah Response
Coaching Model™

④ Implementation

⑤ Celebration

③ Incubation

⑥ Transformation

② Present Situation

① Preferred Future

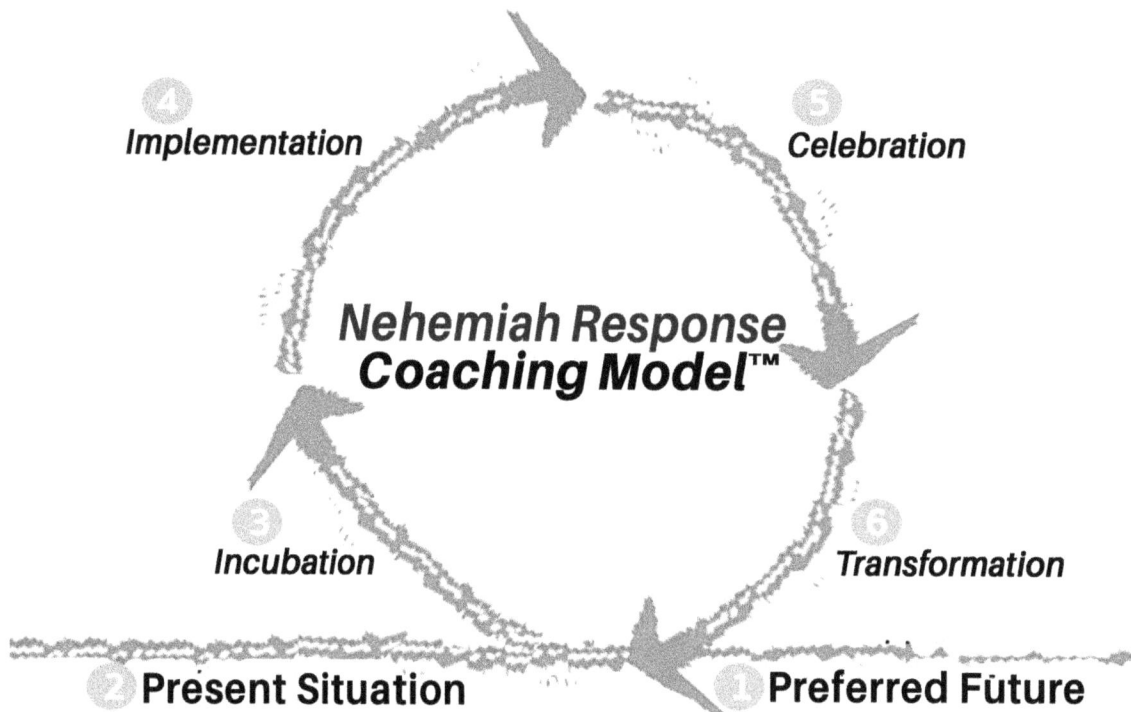

Discipleship session flow...

Suggested elements to incorporate along with the questions on the next page:

- Pray and read scripture.

- Do a check-in on the discipline articles. Ask, "What thoughts did the devotional articles stimulate around the discipline you have been focusing on?"

- Work through the discipline coaching tool.

- Work through the lesson. (If you're in a group or class, you'll work through the lesson)

- Pick the next discipline to focus on and schedule your next session in about three weeks.

Questions to begin with to engage in your disciplee's discipline focus for the past two or three weeks:

1. What was your desire for your discipleship focus the past three weeks? Where would you like to start today?

2. How did you see God show up?

3. What discoveries can you implement for future practice?

4. What will these new practices look like? What challenges could get in your way?

5. So, what do you have to celebrate today?

6. How do you see God working in your life?

Questions to end with to pick the next discipline to focus on:

1. What discipline will you choose to focus on next? What would you like for it to look like in your life?

2. What are things like for you now around this discipline?

3. What are some ways you can practice this discipline moving forward?

4. What will be your first step?

5. What would you like to be able to tell me in three weeks?

6. How will this impact your relationship with God?

You've dedicated the past six months to your discipleship journey; so, **what's next?**

For disciples:

- Continue walking out the Relevant Discipleship Pathway™ one-to-one with another disciple
- Attend a Train the Discipler™ Workshop #1 (emphasis on being a disciple)
- Attend a Train the Discipler™ Workshop #2 (emphasis on making disciples)
- Attend Coach Training to develop your coaching skills taught by Relevant Ministry∗

For pastors and leaders:

- Complete all of the above
- Attend a Certificate in Discipleship Coaching Course taught by Relevant Ministry∗ in partnership with Coaching4Clergy (24 ICF accredited hours)
- Implement Relevant Discipleship into your ministry or group of churches
- Enhance leadership development with coach training and workshops taught by Relevant Ministry∗

Small Groups or Sunday School Classes:

Consider an eleven-week book study in your group or class. The books listed below will immerse you and your group or class in the coaching approach and the discipleship pathway.

- *Nehemiah Response: a coaching model,* Nelson and Pam Roth
- *Relevant Discipleship Pathway: a framework for intentional transformation that multiplies,* Nelson Roth

∗www.relevantministry.org/training

www.ingramcontent.com/pod-product-compliance
Lightning Source LLC
Chambersburg PA
CBHW080518090426
42734CB00015B/3099